Clinical Exercises for Treating Traumatic Stress in Children and Adolescents

of related interest

Cognitive Behavioural Therapy for Child Trauma and Abuse
A Step-by-Step Approach
Jacqueline S. Feather and Kevin R. Ronan
ISBN 978 1 84905 086 9
eISBN 978 0 85700 263 1

Children and Adolescents in Trauma
Creative Therapeutic Approaches
Edited by Chris Nicholson, Michael Irwin and Kedar N. Dwivedi
Foreword by Peter Wilson
ISBN 978 1 84310 437 7
eISBN 978 0 85700 356 0
Part of the Community, Culture and Change series

Therapy To Go
Gourmet Fast Food Handouts for Working with Child, Adolescent and Family Clients
Clare Rosoman
ISBN 978 1 84310 643 2
eISBN 978 1 84642 838 8

Understanding Crisis Therapies
An Integrative Approach to Crisis Intervention and Post Traumatic Stress
Hilda Loughran
ISBN 978 1 84905 032 6
eISBN 978 0 85700 555 7

Empathic Care for Children with Disorganized Attachments
A Model for Mentalizing, Attachment and Trauma-Informed Care
Chris Taylor
Foreword by Peter Fonagy
ISBN 978 1 84905 182 8
eISBN 978 0 85700 398 0

Counselling Skills for Working with Trauma
Healing From Child Sexual Abuse, Sexual Violence and Domestic Abuse
Christiane Sanderson
ISBN 978 1 84905 326 6
eISBN 978 0 85700 743 8

Clinical Exercises for Treating Traumatic Stress in Children and Adolescents

Practical Guidance and Ready-to-use Resources

Damion J. Grasso

Jessica Kingsley *Publishers*
London and Philadelphia

First published in 2014
by Jessica Kingsley Publishers
73 Collier Street
London N1 9BE, UK
and
400 Market Street, Suite 400
Philadelphia, PA 19106, USA

www.jkp.com

Copyright © Damion J. Grasso 2014

Library of Congress Cataloging in Publication Data
A CIP catalog record for this book is available from the Library of Congress

British Library Cataloguing in Publication Data
A CIP catalogue record for this book is available from the British Library

ISBN 978 1 84905 949 7
eISBN 978 0 85700 768 1

Printed and bound in Great Britain by Bell and Bain Ltd, Glasgow

This book is dedicated to my wife, Jennifer Grasso, for being the constant in my life and for holding my hand through the joys and pitfalls it bestows, and to our two daughters, Shianne and Sierra, who keep me in the present, remind me of my priorities, and make each day new and full of joy.

Contents

Acknowledgements

I have numerous current and past mentors to thank for their unselfish interest in contributing to my professional development and career. They have provided me with a strong foundation in child development, experimental science, assessment and diagnostics, cognitive behavioural therapy, and stress and coping. I thank Drs Hugh and Mary Ann Foley for introducing me to the field of psychology while I was a student at Skidmore College and for inspiring me to pursue graduate studies. I thank Dr Joan Kaufman at Yale University School of Medicine for adopting me into her longitudinal study of maltreated children back when I was a Master's student and for continuing to collaborate with me on shared interests.

At the University of Delaware I extend special thanks to several of the psychology faculty for providing a solid doctoral training programme grounded in the clinical science model. I particularly want to acknowledge Dr Robert Simons, my graduate advisor, for his guidance, wisdom and infectious passion for scientific inquiry, as well as Dr Adele Hayes for providing a basic foundation in psychotherapy and for sharing her expert knowledge in therapy process research.

I am grateful to several individuals with whom I had the privilege of collaborating in an effectiveness study of Trauma-Focused Cognitive Behavioural Therapy (TF-CBT). Most significantly, I thank Dr Chuck Webb, a wonderful and sincere mentor and friend who does impeccable work and cares immensely about the population he serves in Delaware. I thank Dr Esther Deblinger, one of the developers of TF-CBT who played an instrumental role in learning about and becoming proficient in the model. I also want to acknowledge Gwen Derr, Beth Joselow, Dr Aileen Fink, Dr Harvey Doppelt, Susan Cycyk and Nancy Widdoes who made the Delaware project possible and also contributed to a state-published TF-CBT workbook, which inspired the concept for this book.

I am grateful to my colleagues and mentors who provided me with superb predoctoral clinical training at the Medical University of South Carolina, and in particular, to the faculty of the National Crime Victims Center, including Drs Ben Saunders, Dean Kilpatrick, Dan Smith, Michael De Arellano, Carla Danielson and Cathy Best.

I want to recognise my current colleagues and collaborators at the University of Connecticut School of Medicine. Most significantly, I thank Dr Julian Ford for providing me unmatched mentoring while I was a postdoctoral fellow and for continuing to offer me guidance and collaborative opportunities, as well as Dr Margaret Briggs-Gowan, for being a wonderful mentor and collaborator.

Finally, I extend my sincerest thanks to the children and families I have had contact with over the years in the numerous clinics and service agencies in which I have had the privilege of providing trauma-informed clinical psychotherapy in the states of Connecticut, Delaware, Pennsylvania and South Carolina. My academic and clinical training, combined with my experience with these children and families, is what made this book a true resource to clinicians serving trauma-exposed children and adolescents.

Preface

This book is the result of several years of working with children, adolescents and adults exposed to adversity, violence and trauma, and consequently struggling with a range of life impairments. I have had the privilege of developing a perspective on the topic of treating trauma-related psychopathology that combines my experiences as an academic researcher, clinician and foster caregiver to a traumatised child. The guidance and exercises in this book surely benefited from this unique combination of roles.

The contents of the book reflect a large body of literature on psychotherapy effectiveness and child and adolescent traumatic stress. Decades of work by pioneers in the field have given rise to efficacious approaches to treating child traumatic stress. My purpose for putting together this book was to provide practical guidance and exercises that reflect the principle components of effective approaches and that are compatible and applicable within the framework of a number of treatment models. In doing so I also strived to bridge the guidance available in manualised treatment protocols to actual practice – providing creative applications and examples on how to customise effective components to the individual needs of the patient. I encourage the end user of this book to extend these applications by exploring other creative approaches to trauma work with children and adolescents. My only caveat is that they do so while still maintaining fidelity to the key principles deemed efficacious by the research literature.

Note: To avoid gender stereotyping, I have used 'she' and 'he' alternately throughout this resource.

PART 1
Getting Started

CHAPTER 1
How to Use this Resource

The purpose of this resource is to supplement existing evidence-based models by providing therapists with practical exercises and activities that are applicable to common treatment components. The intended use of these exercises and activities is by clinicians with sufficient training to be competent in providing these models and working with trauma-exposed children and adolescents. Clinicians should have a Master's-level degree or higher in a clinically relevant field. Importantly, this resource is not intended to replace existing evidence-based models – it is up to the clinician to determine which exercises are compatible with a given model.

The exercises are generally applicable to children and adolescents, ages 8–18. However, some will be more suitable for older children and adolescents and these are pointed out. Further, the language and style of each exercise should be adapted to fit the developmental age of the child or adolescent, as well as individual needs. For simplicity, the remainder of the book uses *child* to refer to both children and adolescents, unless specifically referring to adolescents.

Part 2 then begins with exercises for preparing the child for therapeutic exposure. Most of the existing evidence-based models provide some degree of education about trauma and how it can lead to trauma-related symptoms, as well as an explanation of the rationale of treatment. Many also provide children with skills to better regulate intense emotions and bodily sensations. Children learn techniques to alter their physiological state and to modify perceptions and cognitions – what I refer to as *regulating intense emotional states from the outside in and the inside out*, respectively. These techniques are informed by Cognitive Behavioural Therapy (CBT), which includes recognising one's thoughts and understanding the linkages between emotions, cognitions and behaviours, and mindfulness-based approaches, which use imagery, focused attention and meditation. Part 2 also incorporates elements from family systems and relational therapies including identifying and addressing ineffective social strategies, understanding the value of social support and acquiring and maintaining one's social support network. Next, exercises devoted to helping children to identify healthy and unhealthy aspects of their lifestyle, and to pursue and succeed at healthy lifestyle changes are covered. Part 2 concludes with guidance on introducing children to the idea of increasing their tolerance to distress in the presence of trauma reminders.

Part 3 features exercises that help facilitate therapeutic exposure. These are designed for children presenting with different degrees of avoidant behaviour and different degrees of skills mastery. For example, highly avoidant children may benefit more from low-level or graduated therapeutic exposure, whereas children who demonstrate a readiness to process the trauma memory may be better served with a more intensive therapeutic exposure. This part also includes exercises designed to facilitate therapist-guided or independent in-vivo exposure or therapeutic exposure to avoided places or things outside of the therapy office. Finally, several exercises focus on facilitating cognitive and emotional processing of the trauma memory.

Part 4 centres on working with caregivers. Many of the skills learned and much of the knowledge covered in therapy with the child are also relevant to the caregiver. Other exercises pertain to helping caregivers better manage unwanted behaviour at home. Part 4 also offers guidance on how to engage children and families with significant barriers to treatment. This might include adapting exercises designed for office-based therapy to be conducted at the child's home, school or in the community.

You are encouraged to familiarise yourself with the menu of options featured in this resource so you can choose exercises that fit the individual needs and characteristics of the children you serve. You are also encouraged to use this resource as an inspirational springboard for other creative exercises and techniques. Most exercises have a 'Creative applications' section featuring alternative ways of presenting the material or conducting the exercise. Designing creative exercises also entails expanding your use of technology. Consider using tools such as online applications, illustration software, photo editing software and/or digital video recorders. These will help to engage children and maintain their attention.

Importantly, it is my intention that the exercises be employed in conjunction with an evidence-based model for treating trauma-related problems in children. I tried to incorporate exercises that cover the many different components embedded in these therapies and in the trauma literature. Thus, any adaptations of these exercises or new exercises inspired by this collection should be grounded in evidence-based practice. As influenced by the bulk of the existing literature, much of the information in this book is consistent with a cognitive behavioural approach.

To this end, I hope you enjoy using this resource and also that it enhances your important work with this vulnerable population.

CHAPTER 2
What is Trauma Work?

By the time children reach adolescence most have experienced a stressful event with the potential of causing traumatic stress (Copeland *et al.* 2007). We can refer to these as potentially traumatic events. A fraction of these children develop emotional or behavioural problems because of the trauma exposure. A smaller number struggle with severe and pervasive problems that cut across a number of functional domains (Grasso, Greene and Ford 2013). If children with trauma-related problems are fortunate enough to be identified and referred to treatment, the field of clinical psychology offers a number of effective behavioural approaches with varying degrees of empirical validation. Many of these models share common ingredients and theoretical underpinnings. The purpose of this resource is to offer practical knowledge and exercises that correspond to these shared components so that they can be applied to a number of these approaches. This will allow you to benefit from a non-specific trauma work toolkit, while retaining the freedom to choose the intervention model or approach you feel best fits a particular patient.

The core components or *active ingredients* of psychotherapeutic interventions for trauma-related emotional and behavioural problems include:

- education about trauma and trauma-related problems

- motivation and rationale for treatment

- education about the effects of stress on the brain and body

- physiological techniques to regulate intense emotions

- cognitive techniques to regulate intense emotions

- problem-solving skills

- habituation to the trauma memory

- cognitive and emotional processing of the trauma memory

- habituation to trauma-associated people, places and things in the present

- safety planning

- parenting practices

- establishing a therapeutic alliance with the patient and caregiver.

Below are brief descriptions of each of these components, which are discussed in more detail later in the resource.

Education about trauma and trauma-related problems

Most children and their caregivers have misled beliefs about trauma exposure and its effects. In fact, many people still think of post-traumatic stress disorder (PTSD) mainly as a disorder suffered by soldiers exposed to the atrocities of war. It was only in the past couple of decades that PTSD has been extended to children, and even more recently to young children. Even when individuals are aware that PTSD can happen to children and adolescents, many simply generalise the symptoms typical of combat-related PTSD to children. In fact, it can look very different.

In addition, many individuals have only a cursory understanding of what PTSD symptoms really are. Commonly known symptoms include experiencing *flashbacks* and having intense nightmares. Not only do most people not grasp the full spectrum of symptoms observed in PTSD, they do not understand the developmental differences in symptom presentation of PTSD in young people. These misperceptions can lead to a failure to identify and respond to trauma-related symptoms in children, as well as misguided expectations of what therapy will bring (more on this later). The psychoeducation component of treatment functions to provide an overview of (a) *what potential trauma exposure is*, (b) *statistics about the probability of exposure and development of trauma-related problems*, and (c) *what trauma-related symptoms and PTSD look like in children and adolescents*. The goal is to normalise the child's experiences and the caregiver's concerns, discourage distorted beliefs about trauma exposure that may hinder recovery and progress, and establish realistic expectations for treatment.

Motivation and rationale for treatment

Avoidance is the hallmark symptom of PTSD and is often an obstacle to treatment. Talking about the traumatic event is threatening to the child and may give rise to tremendous resistance. In most cases, the child's caregiver or another authority is the one initiating therapy, not the child. In some cases, this may be the child's first experience with psychotherapy. The therapist's job is to attempt to assuage the child's anxieties about therapy and what it will entail by providing a brief overview of the treatment. This will include an introduction to the idea of and rationale behind therapeutic exposure. Real-life examples and analogies help to convey this to the child.

Caregivers, even if they are the initiators of treatment, may likely be hesitant or sceptical about the therapeutic approach. Many caregivers have avoided discussing the traumatic event for fear of upsetting their child or because they themselves were experiencing trauma-related symptoms from the same traumatic event or one from the past. Further, it is not necessarily intuitive to think that focusing so hard on the thing that is distressing and causing the problems will make the situation better. Caregivers and children want to move past the trauma, not dwell on it. Thus, the therapist explains why focusing intensely on the trauma memory while in therapy will facilitate moving beyond the trauma.

Stress on the brain and body

Understanding how the brain and body respond to normal and traumatic stress helps children and their caregivers put the child's symptoms into context. It demystifies traumatic stress and links symptoms to more tangible problems in how the brain and body are dealing with the stress. It normalises them. This knowledge also reinforces the rationale for engaging in therapeutic exposure. If children can conceptualise the therapeutic exposure as *training* the brain and body not to be *reactive* to the memory of the traumatic event, they may be more likely to engage in and tolerate the therapy. This knowledge will also help to inform skills on how to use our understanding of how the body works to relax and reduce anxiety.

Physiological techniques to regulate intense emotions

Teaching the child to develop the ability to regulate bodily reactions to stress can help in better coping with stress on a day-to-day basis, as well as tolerating therapeutic exposure and processing of the traumatic memory. Bodily reactions can be frightening and overwhelming. If children learn to temper these reactions and exert some control over them using breathing or other relaxation techniques, then these reactions become less obstructive. Commonly taught exercises include deep breathing (or *belly* breathing), muscle tension relaxation and mindfulness techniques. The goal is for children to establish a menu of options with which they can draw upon in stressful situations.

Cognitive techniques to regulate intense emotions

Like physiological techniques to regulate intense emotion, cognitive techniques help the child to better cope with everyday stress, as well as to tolerate thinking and talking about the traumatic event in session. You might think of physiological techniques as working from the *outside in* (i.e., the body to the brain) and cognitive techniques as working from the *inside out* (i.e., the brain to the body). The former method can be conceptualised as the body signalling the brain to change cognitions and feelings, whereas in the latter situation, the brain is signalling the body to change its physical state. In reality, the processes are more dynamic than that, but it is a helpful way of thinking about it. Cognitive techniques include things such as *self-talk*, identifying and falsifying unhelpful thoughts, and paying attention to thoughts triggered by trauma-related stimuli.

Problem-solving skills

Developing a skill set for solving problems involves adopting a template of steps the child can refer to when faced with a situation that demands some kind of action. The template should be simple and easy to remember. It is a tool for young people to evaluate information in a more logical and systematic way. The template is only useful if the child has fully adopted it and it has become part of procedural memory, like riding a bike. To do so, the child must practise using these skills over several iterations.

Habituation to the trauma memory

Through the process of repeated exposure to the traumatic memory the child begins to habituate to it – meaning that the child's body becomes less and less reactive to reminders of the trauma. Habituation is a common mechanism across several anxiety disorders. Whereas the PTSD patient is habituating to a traumatic memory, however, the patient with panic disorder or social phobia is habituating to bodily sensations or social stimuli, respectively. The common thread is that the patient is willingly putting himself into a situation in which he will encounter that which causes the distress.

There are a number of different ways to conduct therapeutic exposure with children. In Prolonged Exposure (Foa and Rothbaum 1988), the therapist facilitates Imaginal Exposure, whereby the adolescent is asked to close his eyes and retell the traumatic event from start to finish, in first person, present tense, and to do so repeatedly for 45 minutes. In other models, including Trauma-Focused Cognitive Behavioural Therapy (TF-CBT; Cohen, Mannarino and Deblinger 2006), children and adolescents work with the therapist to develop a written narrative of the traumatic event, and it is the act of writing or dictating the narrative that functions to expose the child to the trauma memory. The therapist must make other decisions including how gradual to make the therapeutic exposure (i.e., slowly increasing the intensity of the exposure across sessions), when to switch the focus to another aspect of the traumatic event or another traumatic event entirely, and when to temper the exposure within session, among other things. These are discussed in more detail later.

Cognitive and emotional processing of the trauma memory

In conjunction with or after therapeutic exposure the therapist works with the child to help him to process the trauma memory. *Processing* is a broad notion that can be confusing for therapists and patients alike. Whereas information processing means perceiving and interpreting environmental stimuli, processing the trauma memory means pulling up the memory and re-analysing it in order to gain a better understanding of the trauma and what it means in the context of one's life, increasing one's personal control of the memory, and organising the way in which one makes sense of oneself, others and the world.

There is some evidence that therapeutic exposure and *activation* of the cognitions, physiological sensations and emotions associated with the trauma is necessary to process the trauma memory. In other words, activation of these components *activates* the trauma memory (as memory is a combination of these things) and allows the patient to add new information to the memory *file* and to re-consolidate the memory (Brewin and Holmes 2003). When re-consolidated, the memory retains the new information (e.g., different way of interpreting what happened) so that it is retrieved the next time the memory is activated. There are numerous ways to help patients to process the trauma memory, which are discussed later.

Habituation to trauma-associated people, places and things in the present

This is often referred to as in-vivo (i.e., *in real life*) exposure. It deals with the child's avoidance of people, places, things and situations that trigger unwanted thoughts or feelings associated with the trauma. This type of therapeutic exposure is most similar to the kind used to treat individuals with agoraphobia, social phobia or specific phobias. Children are subjected to the stimuli that trigger the unwanted thoughts and feelings. Through repeated exposure, the unwanted thoughts and feelings become less and less until the association is no longer strong enough to elicit avoidance behaviour.

Safety planning

Safety planning involves planning for a safe future – preventing trauma exposure insomuch as it can be prevented. Violence-exposed children and adolescents are exponentially more likely than their non-exposed peers to be re-exposed (Finkelhor, Ormrod and Turner 2007). The goal of safety planning is to reduce these odds. Safety planning depends on the child's situation. It may involve reducing high-risk behaviour (e.g., runaway behaviour, alcohol or substance misuse), having a specific plan of action in the event of future domestic violence exposure or realising the importance of telling a trusted adult in the event of sexual assault. Safety planning can be conceptualised as increasing a child's protective resources in the event the child finds himself facing a challenging situation in the future.

Parenting practices

This critical component aims to help caregivers to best support the child through the process of recovery, as well as to manage difficult behaviours at home. Much of the progress a child makes in therapy depends on the translation of what is learned in session to his home, school and community environment. Caregivers face a significant challenge in therapy. They must often make a shift in the way they have been treating the child's trauma. Many caregivers avoid talking about the trauma for fear of upsetting their children. Others are so distraught by the trauma that they may become deeply upset in front of their child. Thus, the child and caregiver's avoidance of the trauma material often reinforces the other, as the child does not want to upset the caregiver and vice versa.

The therapist's job is to teach the caregiver to support the child's trauma work by encouraging him to engage in therapeutic exposure with the therapist, and by inviting the child freely to discuss the trauma, or other aspects of treatment, at home. Essentially, the parent is taught to adopt the principles of trauma recovery and implement these in the home environment.

The other component involves helping the caregiver to manage difficult behaviours. The traumatised child can pose significant challenges at home and in school. Indeed, several symptoms of PTSD can present as disruptive behaviour problems. Further, it is common for the act of therapeutic exposure temporarily to exacerbate symptoms given that the trauma memory is especially salient during this period and the child is fluctuating between actively processing the memory to employing maladaptive avoidance strategies. The therapist should prepare the caregiver for anticipating and effectively accommodating this period.

Establishing a therapeutic alliance with the patient and caregiver

While establishing a therapeutic alliance is important across all types of psychotherapy, it is particularly critical in the area of trauma work. Children and adolescents must feel comfortable and safe with the therapist in order to push past their strong avoidance and do what seems unnatural to them – face the traumatic memory. Building an alliance with a young patient may take time. Some children will need more time and effort than others before they are ready to work with the therapist, and there is not a prescription for how to do this. The way a patient responds to you (and vice versa) is multifactorial. Also critical is the therapist's working relationship with caregivers. It is important that caregivers trust the therapist's judgement and feel comfortable with the therapist–child relationship. Further, the therapist must invest the caregiver in the principles of the therapy for him to *bring it home* and wholly apply it to the child.

CHAPTER 3
Evidence-based Models

Evidence for the efficacy of TF-CBT has been demonstrated in a number of randomised controlled trials (RCTs) and has been deemed *supported and efficacious* based on current standards (Cohen *et al.* 2006). TF-CBT has led to significantly reduced symptoms of PTSD, depression, dissociation and sexualised behaviour, and increased social competence in sexually abused children relative to children in a wait list control or comparison control group (Cohen *et al.* 2010). In one study, more than two-thirds of children who received TF-CBT no longer met criteria for PTSD post-treatment compared to only about half of children who received client-centred therapy (Cohen *et al.* 2000, 2004; Deblinger *et al.* 2006a, 2006b, 2010, 2011; DeVoe 2009; Mannarino *et al.* 2012). Research also suggests that the therapeutic effects of TF-CBT are maintained over time (Cohen *et al.* 2004). In fact, in one study, children who received TF-CBT continued to show reductions in symptoms two years after they completed the therapy (Cohen, Mannarino and Knudsen 2005; Deblinger, Steer and Lippmann 1999).

Several experts have worked hard to implement and test TF-CBT within community-based mental health systems and special populations. In one community-based effectiveness study, TF-CBT demonstrated significant reductions in symptoms of PTSD and internalising behaviour problems in children with a variety of trauma types and from vulnerable populations: child welfare, juvenile justice and crisis services (Deblinger *et al.* 1999). Bigfoot and Schmidt (2010) developed and validated an adaptation of TF-CBT for American Indians and Alaskan Natives called Honoring Children, Mending the Circle (HC-MC), which blends traditional cultural teachings with the model components. Finally, De Arellano and colleagues (2005) have modified TF-CBT to be conducted in the child's community, in or around the home, to help underserved populations who face significant barriers to treatment and over-represented families who end up dropping out of treatment.

For children with co-occurring traumatic stress and significant disruptive behaviour problems the developers of TF-CBT suggest incorporating a functional behaviour analysis to determine the function of the behaviour and to focus on the problems most pertinent to the family (Cohen, Berliner and Mannarino 2010). While developing a problem list for managing and prioritising a family's concerns is not a new concept in psychology (Woody *et al.* 2003), the practice is sometimes lost in more directive, evidence-based treatment models with pre-selected standardised measures of symptoms and specific objectives already decided.

A less gradual exposure-based model with efficacy for treating adults with PTSD, Prolonged Exposure, has been adapted for use with adolescents (Foa, Chrestman and Gilboa-Schechtman 2009). Prolonged Exposure is a manualised treatment that consists of 9–12 sessions, each lasting about 90 minutes. Introductory sessions cover psychoeducation about PTSD and treatment rationale. The remainder involves repeated Imaginal Exposure in session and assignment of in-vivo exposure out of session. Adolescents are instructed to close their eyes and provide a spoken narrative of the traumatic event in the first person, present tense. The adolescent is encouraged to use as much detail as possible, paying attention to what she had seen, heard, smelled, touched or tasted, as well as to what she was thinking and feeling at the time. If the adolescent completes the narrative before the 45 minutes are up, she is instructed to start again from the beginning, so that in a single session she might go through multiple iterations. In one RCT, two times as many adolescents receiving Prolonged Exposure no longer met criteria for PTSD post-treatment compared to adolescents who received a comparison treatment (Foa, Huppert and Cahill 2006). Treatment gains were maintained more than a year later.

Cognitive Processing Therapy (CPT; Resick and Schnicke 1992) originated from work with female survivors of sexual trauma, but has also been applied to adolescents. CPT is comprised of three key elements: psychoeducation about PTSD and information-processing theory, therapeutic exposure and cognitive therapy. The therapeutic exposure in CPT is achieved through writing assignments. Adolescents complete writing assignments that pertain to the trauma memory and the patient's life. The cognitive therapy piece involves identifying thoughts and emotions, challenging unhealthy thoughts and beliefs and specifically targeting beliefs about safety, trust, power, self-esteem and intimacy. While there has been more research on the efficacy of CPT in adult as opposed to child and adolescent populations, CPT appears to work for adolescents as well. In one study, adolescents who completed CPT showed significantly greater reductions in PTSD, depression and general anxiety symptoms than young people in a wait list control condition (Aderka *et al.* 2011).

Trauma Affect Regulation: Guide for Education and Therapy (TARGET; Ford and Cruz 2006) is a versatile 4- to 12-session intervention that does not involve therapeutic exposure, but rather focuses on restoring emotion regulation following trauma. It is a manualised, evidence-based treatment for adolescents and adults that incorporates psychoeducation and behavioural exercises designed to enhance adaptive emotion recognition and expression, cognitive reappraisal of emotion-related beliefs, and arousal modulation prior to, during or instead of trauma memory processing. TARGET begins with psychoeducation, which links emotional, behavioural, school and relational problems to a shift in the brain's interconnections between an *alarm centre* (i.e., the brain's stress response centre) with information retrieval (i.e., the brain's filing system) and executive functions (i.e., the brain's thinking centre).

The use of this biological model to explain traumatic stress and associated problems provides a de-stigmatising rationale for overcoming dysregulated emotional and behavioural systems by strengthening the brain's filing and thinking centres and resetting the brain's alarm system (Ford and Cruz 2006). In essence, the patient shifts from a *survival* brain to a *learning* brain. TARGET engages patients in learning a seven-step sequence for focusing thinking that draws on skills taught in CBT, mindfulness and experiential approaches. The goal is not to modify the patient's thinking but to demonstrate to the patient that she is capable of deliberately using the ability to think systematically and clearly to achieve balance.

There are several group-based models, and most take a CBT approach. For example, Multi-Modality Trauma Treatment (MMTT; March *et al.* 1998) is an 18-week, manualised group CBT intervention for children and adolescents exposed to single traumatic events. The treatment involves psychoeducation, development of a trauma narrative, muscle relaxation, breathing exercises, interpersonal problem solving for anger control and development of positive self-talk and relapse prevention. Evaluation of the MMTT resulted in more than a 50 per cent reduction in PTSD symptoms post-treatment and nearly 90 per cent reduction at a six-month follow-up. Another example, a shorter, ten-session, group-based intervention using similar CBT techniques, resulted in an 86 per cent reduction in PTSD symptoms for children who received the intervention compared to the control group (Stein *et al.* 2003).

Finally, a number of school-based models exist. A recent review of the literature identified several studies providing evidence that school-based models do a good job of reducing PTSD symptoms, showing medium to large effect sizes (Rolfsnes and Idsoe 2011). One of these models, Cognitive Behavioural Intervention for Trauma in Schools (CBITS), demonstrated efficacy in reducing PTSD symptoms and resulted in a much higher completion rate than TF-CBT (Jaycox *et al.* 2010), likely related to the familiarity and close proximity of schools to the families of the children. The limitations of a school-based setting, however, prevent a more individualised approach and one that incorporates therapeutic exposure.

CHAPTER 4
Making a Problem List and Monitoring Progress

The practice of developing a problem list for managing and prioritising the child and family's primary concerns is sometimes lost in more directive, evidence-based treatments with pre-selected standardised measures of symptoms and specific milestones already laid out. Developing a list of the child's difficulties with the child and his caregiver helps to focus on the child's needs and expectations. The problem list functions as kind of a *to do list* that can be referenced and updated as the child progresses through treatment (Woody *et al.* 2003). Much of the problem list may directly overlap with trauma-related symptoms. Others may be associated with the trauma more indirectly or reflect functional impairment that is a consequence of PTSD symptoms (e.g., few social contacts, loneliness, marijuana use).

When developing the problem list it is important to make each item as concrete and specific as possible. For example, if the caregiver states, 'My child is disliked by other kids,' you might ask, 'What specifically makes your child disliked by other kids?' or 'How do you know that?' in order to arrive at a behaviour that is then observable and measurable. After collaboratively developing the problem list with the child and caregiver, you can talk about how each may or may not overlap or relate to the trauma and PTSD symptoms. Then, discuss with the child and caregiver how they would define successful treatment. That is, establish realistic expectations and a sense of how treatment benefit will be determined.

Monitoring and tracking progress and using these data to provide feedback to children and families is often talked about but seldom done. Establishing a system of collecting repeated assessment data over the course of therapy and monitoring symptom change makes it possible to define and regularly examine measurable and quantifiable goals. Regular child and caregiver feedback on symptom change can inspire optimism and motivate children and their caregivers to continue with therapy.

The first exercise that follows provides guidelines for creating a problem list. The second exercise describes a simple system for quantifying and monitoring symptoms of traumatic stress over the course of therapy.

HOW TO CREATE THE PROBLEM LIST

Goals

- To identify child and caregiver perceptions of functional impairment.
- To delineate a list of specific problems to address in treatment.

Procedure

1. A good approach is to meet with the child and caregiver separately when making the problem list, then bring them together to come to a consensus as to what the final list will entail. This is an unstructured assessment activity; however, be prepared to help the child and caregiver refine each problem so that it is concrete and measurable.

2. Explain the purpose of the problem list.

   What I want to do now is to ask you to make a list of possible problems you see in your life right now. This list will help us to decide how best to work together and will help us to figure out some goals. I will ask your [caregiver] to do the same so we can bring together both points of view. Okay?

3. When making the list, use Socratic questioning (e.g., 'What makes you think this?' 'What is another way of thinking about this?' 'What do you think other people think about this?') to refine each of the problems so that they are concrete and measurable.

[Child]	*My mother doesn't listen to me any more.*
[Therapist]	*How do you know this?*
[Child]	*She always assumes the worst and I can't get a word in.*
[Therapist]	*Can you think of an example?*
[Child]	*Uh, yeah – the other night I got home later than I said I would and my mother had a fit about it. She didn't even hear me out. I was trying to tell her that my friend's car wouldn't start and she wouldn't have it. She just said I wasn't going out with my friends again this week.*
[Therapist]	*Why do you think she responded that way?*
[Child]	*She's just always angry at me. She doesn't trust me.*
[Therapist]	*Did she always not trust you or has she lost trust in you?*
[Child]	*I guess she lost trust in me. I've been making some mistakes. But she should still listen to me sometimes.*
[Therapist]	*So do you just want her to listen to you or do you want her to trust you more and maybe believe what you're saying is true?*
[Child]	*Trust me more.*
[Therapist]	*Okay, so what should we put down as a problem?*

[Child]   My mum doesn't trust me.

[Therapist]   Remember though, we want to make it something that you can work on. How can we phrase it so that the problem starts with 'I' or 'My'?

[Child]   I lost my mother's trust.

[Therapist]   Good.

4. Create the caregiver's list, which can focus both on the child's behaviour (e.g., 'My child…'), as well as the caregiver's (e.g., 'I don't spend enough time with my child').

5. Bring the child and caregiver together to discuss the lists and establish a unified problem list. Use the problem list to set some goals and determine how to measure progress towards those goals. See below.

Example problem:

Child problem:	I lost my mother's trust in me.
Caregiver problem:	My son has told many lies and so I have lost trust in him.
Modified problem:	Telling lies has caused my mother not to believe what I tell her.
Treatment goal:	To earn back my mother's trust by telling the truth and following through with what I say.
Measurement:	Mother's weekly rating (1–10) of trustworthiness.

6. Develop a simple method for keeping track of session-by-session changes in the identified problem areas. Figure 4.1 is an example of a simple chart maintained by hand. Notice that the example in Figure 4.1 is labelled *trustworthiness* rather than *untrustworthiness*. Try to focus on the *positive* behaviour as opposed to the *negative*.

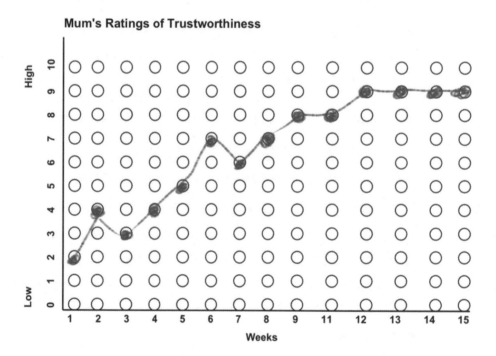

FIGURE 4.1 EXAMPLE OF PROGRESS TRACKER

Creative applications

- Use computer software to create graphically appealing tracking charts. I find that anything done on a computer is more engaging for children. See Figure 4.2 for some examples.

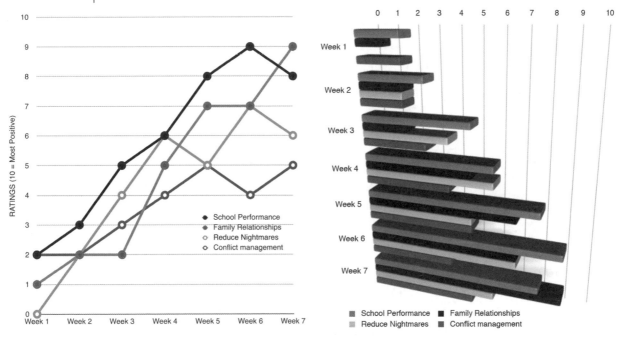

Example 1

Example 2

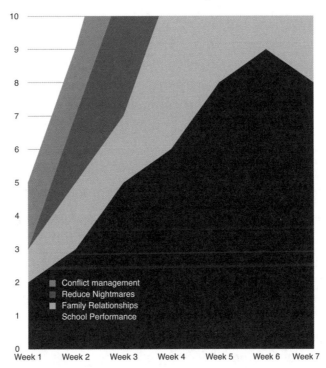

Example 3

FIGURE 4.2 EXAMPLES OF COMPUTER-GENERATED PROBLEM TRACKERS

TRACKING TRAUMA-RELATED SYMPTOMS

Goals

- To establish a simple baseline measure of trauma-related symptoms that can be tracked over time.
- To introduce the method of tracking symptoms across treatment.
- To begin to familiarise the child and caregiver to trauma-related symptoms.

Procedure

1. Print the 'Simple Symptom Checker' and 'Simple Symptom Tracker' worksheets.

2. Explain that the purpose of the exercise is to identify and track trauma-related symptoms over the course of the programme.

    As the reason for coming to see me is to reduce the problems you are having related to [the trauma] I want to make sure that we actually do that. The way that we can do that is to measure how much the trauma-related problems or symptoms are reduced over time. It's as simple as counting up the number of symptoms you have now and see if that number goes down over the course of our working together. To make this easy I have a worksheet that will help us to check off the problems and take a total count.

3.   Give the instructions.

    Okay, so the instructions tell you to check off the problems on the page that you think affect any of these following things. [Read the list.] If a symptom affects one or more of those things, that means it is interfering with your day-to-day activities and functioning and that it is worth fixing. So, there are 18 problems. Let's go through each one and see if it has an effect on one of the items at the top. [For younger children, go through the list together. For older children, you may let them check the problems off on their own.]

4. Introduce the child and caregiver to the 'Simple Symptom Tracker' worksheet (or whatever method you decide to use to track symptoms over time).

    Okay, good. Now let's count them up. [Pause.] I count ten. Remember that number for a minute. Now I want to show you what I call the 'Simple Symptom Tracker'. This is where we can record the total number of problems and track this number over time. On the left side we have the number of symptoms (y-axis) and the bottom line (x-axis) is divided by weeks. As this is the first week, let's follow the line from week 1 up to the number 10 on the y-axis and make a small circle. Next week when we do this we will put the total number of symptoms on the next line that represents week 2. After we have a bunch of weeks plotted, we can draw a line and look at how the symptoms are changing over time.

Name: _____   Start Date: _____ / _____ / _____

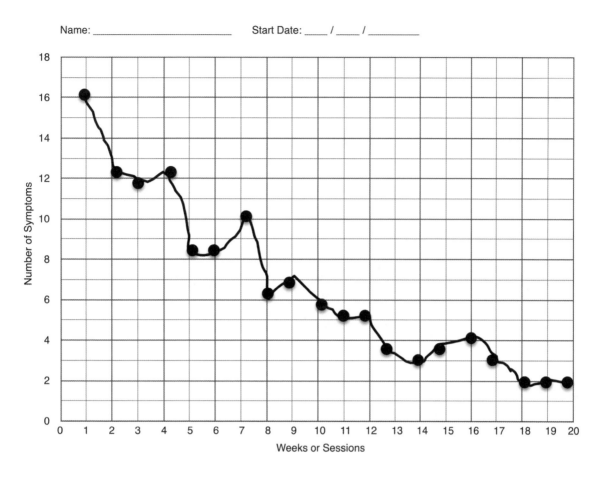

FIGURE 4.3 EXAMPLE OF A SIMPLE SYMPTOM TRACKER

5. Explain that symptom counts may go up and down by a little each week because of different circumstances that come up. Thus, while a decrease in symptoms is the ultimate goal, the pattern will likely not be completely linear.

6. Use the tracker to show the child and caregiver the pattern of change over time. This can be a motivator and tangible evidence that the therapy is working.

PART 2

Preparing Children for Trauma Work

CHAPTER 5
Enhancing Social and Personal Resources

Measuring symptoms is not enough wholly to understand and conceptualise the trauma-exposed child referred to your practice. What is lacking is information about a child's existing protective resources (i.e., What does this child possess that will foster progress and recovery?) and outstanding risk factors (i.e., What can get in the way of this child's progress and recovery in treatment?). This information is critical to develop a personalised and comprehensive treatment plan. Factors associated with resiliency in the face of trauma and worth thinking about include social support, positive self-perception and healthy coping strategies (Bonanno, Westphal and Mancini 2011; Rutter 2013).

Social support

Deficient social support has been identified as one of the most powerful predictors of PTSD in two respected reviews of the research literature (Brewin, Andrews and Valentine 2000; Ozer *et al.* 2008). Social support may contribute to a child's ability to regulate intense emotions associated with the traumatic experience (Charuvastra and Cloitre 2008) and might facilitate recovery from trauma by fostering the perception that the child is part of a solid social network, challenging perceptions that the world is hostile and others are untrustworthy. The perception that one belongs to a safe and protective social network may also promote greater use of healthy, non-avoidant coping strategies by providing a secure base from which to confront the trauma memory. The exercises in this chapter facilitate children's exploration of their social networks and perception of social support, and enable them to act on opportunities to acquire social support, as well as to maintain their social resources over time. A specific emphasis is on improving the child–caregiver relationship.

Positive perceptions of self

Another characteristic associated with resilience involves having a positive perception of self. One facet of this is *self-esteem*, defined as one's attitude towards the self as competent and worthy of respect and acceptance from others (Rosenberg *et al.* 1995). Self-esteem is associated with a reduced risk of developing PTSD and has been shown to predict psychological wellbeing more generally (Bonanno 2008). It is a key element in the personality construct of hardiness, defined as perceiving life events as manageable, and challenges as opportunities for growth (Vogt *et al.* 2008). Another facet of having a positive perception of self is *perceived self-control*, which is protective in the face of extreme stress in that individuals high on this quality are more likely to retain healthy self-cognitions and attributions than view the self as incompetent and less efficacious after the trauma (Foa *et al.* 2006). One of the goals of trauma-focused treatment is to enhance one's sense of self-control when confronting the trauma memory.

Coping strategies

Use of effective coping strategies is another factor that influences individuals' reactions to trauma and extreme stress (Schnider, Elhai and Gray 2007), and can help individuals better tolerate therapeutic exposure. Coping strategies have been described as being approach or avoidance-focused (Folkman and Moskowitz 2004; Taylor and Stanton 2007). Approach-focused coping strategies are action-oriented and involve advancing toward the stressor or problem, whereas avoidance-focused coping strategies, characteristic of PTSD, evade the stressor or problem (Littleton *et al.* 2007). Avoidance-focused coping strategies, such as the use of distraction (e.g., flipping the channels on the television), may work in the short term, but are problematic and maladaptive in the long term (Littleton *et al.* 2007). Avoidance-focused coping impedes one's ability to reconcile the information learned from having experienced the trauma with pre-existing beliefs and present experiences – perpetuating the debilitating distress felt when exposed to trauma reminders. In contrast, approach-focused coping strategies are associated with both physical and psychological health benefits (Taylor and Stanton 2007), as well as progress in exposure-based therapies.

Identifying, enhancing and acquiring resources

A useful theory to help guide this section is the Conservation of Resources (COR) theory (Hobfoll 1989), which describes a pattern whereby exposure to trauma precipitates an initial loss of resources, including instrumental resources such as transportation and healthcare, as well as internal or psychological resources such as self-efficacy, self-competence and humour. Research in the field has shown that resource loss predicts traumatic stress above and beyond the effect of trauma exposure alone (Hobfoll 2001). Resource gain following trauma, accomplished by replacing or substituting the loss, reduces this risk (Hobfoll 2001). Thus, resilient outcomes following trauma are associated with individuals' ability to optimise or enhance their remaining resources and/or compensate for the resource loss by acquiring new resources.

Efforts to salvage and enhance remaining resources, as well as to acquire new resources, however, are costly, and demand mobilisation of existing resources, which many traumatised individuals lack (Hobfoll 2001). While those individuals with sufficient resources may be proactive in terms of maintaining, acquiring and enhancing resources, those who lack them may be particularly vulnerable to additional loss (Hobfoll 2001). Moreover, individuals who successfully recover from the trauma-related loss may actually build stronger resources, including coping strategies, than those who have not experienced resource loss and never had the need to strengthen them (Grasso, Cohen *et al.* 2012; Hobfoll 2001). In contrast, individuals with multiple losses may fall prey to what has been called a *loss spiral* – an acceleration of the loss of resources and deleterious consequences (Hobfoll 2001).

Given that children presenting for trauma-focused therapy are likely to have experienced significant resource loss, and likely to lack the ability to enhance remaining resources or acquire new ones on their own, it is up to the therapist to educate the child and caregiver about the importance of these resources and to help them to re-establish sufficient resources. The following exercises were designed to facilitate this goal.

PRIORITISING PREREQUISITE SKILLS AND RESOURCES

Goals

- To identify deficits in skills and resources necessary for trauma work.
- To make choices about which skills and resources to prioritise for pre-exposure development.

Procedure

1. Determining what the child needs to optimise her ability to engage in and benefit from therapeutic exposure and trauma memory processing requires some preliminary information gathering and assessment. You can glean much of this from your initial interview with the child and caregiver. There are also a number of standardised assessment instruments you can use to measure strengths and difficulties more comprehensively. Use the items in Table 5.1 to help to compile and prioritise the skills and resources you see as most important prerequisites for therapeutic exposure and trauma memory processing.

2. Engage the child and caregiver (separately or together) in ranking the skills and resources in Table 5.1 from most proficient to least proficient. One idea is to put these items on index cards and have both the child and caregiver put them in rank order. By including the child and caregiver you are also introducing them, as well as including them, in the initial treatment planning.

3. Review the prioritised (i.e., lowest ranked) items and discuss your intention for focusing on these areas in subsequent sessions.

TABLE 5.1 PRIORITISING PREREQUISITE SKILLS AND RESOURCES

Child attributes	Child rank	Caregiver rank	Clinician rank	Module
1. Uses skills to calm down in stressful situations.				
2. Has a sufficient vocabulary for communicating the way she feels.				
3. Identifies what triggers her feelings.				
4. Seeks help from others when she feels upset.				
5. Uses problem-solving skills to approach problems.				
6. Can identify and communicate her thoughts.				
7. Does not use alcohol or substances to cope with problems or feelings.				
8. Recognises her weaknesses.				
9. Understands that trauma reminders affect the way she feels.				
10. Seeks help from others when she has a problem she cannot solve.				
11. Can reframe situations to reach a more positive outlook.				
12. Identifies long-term goals.				
13. Identifies short-term goals.				
14. Plans for the future.				
15. Accepts things she cannot change.				

IDENTIFYING EXISTING SOCIAL RESOURCES

Goals

- To assess the quality of the child's social support network.
- To teach the child the importance of social support in coping with stress.
- To help the child to identify her social resources.
- To encourage the child to use her social resources.

Procedure

1. Create several descriptive categories of ways that people can be important to us. These should include examples of both *emotional* and *instrumental* support. Category examples are provided in Figure 5.1. The child can help to develop the categories and descriptions; however, it is a good idea to have several already available prior to the session. This way you can supplement the child's list if you need to.

2. The objective is to match the people the child identifies in her life with the various categories. Each person may fit more than one category. Put each category title and description on an index card. Instruct the child to think of as many people in her life that fit each category and write their first name or initials on the back of the card.

3. Introduce the goals of the session in lay language and set the agenda. You might write the goals out on a dry erase board or piece of paper to serve as a visual reminder.

   I want to talk to you today about ways that other people are important to us and helpful in dealing with stress or solving problems. I also want to get a sense of the people in your life and how they are important to you in a number of different ways. Humans are social creatures. We need other people in all sorts of ways. Because other people are so important to us I want to spend most of our meeting today talking about that. [Pause.] *How do you think people can be helpful to us?* [Wait for child's response and engage in discussion.]

4. With your pre-established categories in mind, engage the child in coming up with specific categories that reflect ways in which people are important. You could use index cards, poster board or a computer word processing programme.

   Let's make up some specific categories that will cover all of the ways that people are important to us. Let's put each of the groups we come up with on one of these index cards. [Create categories and discuss each.]

5. Ask the child to look over the categories and to think of all of the people in her life that might fit into the categories. As the child thinks of different people, have her write down their first names or initials somewhere proximal to the category. If you use index cards, you can put the names on the backs of the cards. The nice thing about index cards is that the child can take them home and reference them as needed.

Now what I'd like you to do is to think of all of the people currently in your life that fit into these different groups. What you can do is put their first name or their initials on the back of the group's index card. You might see that some people will fit into more than one group.

6. The number of people the child identifies and the extent to which the categories are well represented will give you a sense of the quality of the child's social support network (Goal 1).

7. Explain the importance of emotional and instrumental support during times of stress and have the child provide personal examples (Goal 2). Which people on the list actually provided the child with emotional or instrumental support in the recent past? Ask the child whether she can identify areas of strengths and weaknesses and help the child to recognise these (Goal 3). Are there people in the child's life that bring her down or make problems worse for her? Which categories or domains have the fewest people listed? How can the child enhance these areas? Have the child recall situations in which she may have relied on the support of one or more of the people on the list (Goal 4). Were there times in the child's life when emotional or instrumental support would have been helpful?

Sample Categories

- People you could talk to about something very personal or private.

- People you could depend on if you needed to borrow something like a book, money, a video game, or something else.

- People you would go to if you needed advice or help solving a problem.

- People who would let you know when you are doing a good job or remind you of your positive qualities.

- People you could rely on to provide a helping hand or help you to do something that might require time and energy.

- People you would spend time with to relax and have a good time.

- People you could rely on to let you know when you are doing something wrong or suggest doing something a different way.

- People you look up to as role models or people who you admire.

FIGURE 5.1 IDENTIFYING THE CHILD'S SOCIAL NETWORK

Creative applications

1. *Circles* (see Figure 5.2). Draw a circle in the middle of a blank sheet of paper or poster board. The circle in the middle of the worksheet represents the child. The child thinks of people in her life and draws a circle for each person in relation to her own circle to reflect how close she feels to that person (e.g., an overlapping circle may indicate a very close relationship). Colour code the categories and have the child add corresponding colours to each individual circle to represent the associated categories.

I am going to draw a circle in the middle of this paper. Let's say that the circle represents you. [Put the child's name in it.] Now, what I'd like you to do is to think of all of the people currently in your life and draw a circle for each of them. Put the circles close or far away from your circle depending on how much support they provide you and how close you feel to them. So, someone really close to you might overlap with your circle. Someone not very close to you may be near the edge of the paper. [After completion.] Great job. Now, remember those categories we came up with? Let's choose a colour for each one. [Do this.] Now, I want you to think about these individuals and what categories they might fall into. For each category they fit into, add that category's colour to their circle.

2. *Sixty seconds.* Tell the child she has 60 seconds to write as many names of the people in her life as possible on a sheet of paper. After the time is up, have the child identify the categories that pertain to each individual. You might do this by colour coding the categories and having the child circle the names with corresponding colours.

    Let me challenge you. See this piece of paper? I want to see how many names of people in your life you can think of in 60 seconds or less. You can write their first name or initials. Are you ready? Go. [After completion.] Great job. Now, remember those categories we came up with? Let's choose a colour for each one. [Do this.] Now, I want you to think about these individuals and what categories they might fall into. For each category they fit into, circle their name or initials with that category's colour.

FIGURE 5.2 CIRCLES EXAMPLE

After the session

1. Make a note indicating what you have learned about the child's social support network. Is it a relative strength? Weakness? If it is a weakness, are there ways you can help the child to strengthen it? You might incorporate this into the child's treatment goals. Also, you might consider discussing this material with the caregiver, as she may have insight into the child's social support network and/or may join in working on improving the child's social support. At the very least, you will want to emphasise to the caregiver the importance of social support, and especially the parent–child relationship.

2. Think about ways in which you might quantify the quality of the child's social support network. There are a number of social support measures available; however, you could do something as simple as count the number of positive social supports in each of the categories that you and the child had generated. Then, you might repeat that portion of this module at a later point in therapy to determine if the child's social support network has increased.

BUILDING SOCIAL RESOURCES

Goals

- To identify and reduce barriers of social support.
- To teach the child ways of establishing social resources.
- To emphasise the value of providing social support.

Procedure

1. Generate a list of important things to consider when developing a social relationship with someone. This could be making a new friend, getting to know a new teacher or further developing an existing relationship with a friend, teacher or other person. Some possible things to consider are provided in Figure 5.3.

Things to Consider

- What kind of person would I get along with?
- Where are some good places to meet people?
- How do I greet someone new?
- What could I talk about?
- Show that you are a good listener.
- How do I finish the conversation when I'm done?

- Pay attention to your body language.
- Make good eye contact.
- Stay in touch with them by returning phone calls, texts and emails.
- Accept people's help when they offer it.
- Respect others' needs and wishes.
- Say thank you.

FIGURE 5.3 BUILDING SOCIAL RESOURCES

2. Introduce the goals of the exercise. Ask the child to help you to make a list of things that are important to think about when making a new friend. Work with the child to define each of the items on the list.

   Today I thought we might talk about what it takes to build and keep a relationship with someone. This could be a friend, girlfriend/boyfriend, parent, teacher, mentor, coach, or brother or sister. First I want to focus on what kinds of things are important to think about in the beginning of a relationship. What is important when making a new friend? [Let child respond.] *Okay, great.*

3. Then ask the child to make a list of things that are important when keeping or maintaining a friend or getting to know a friend better.

Now, what types of things are important in keeping existing friends? Some of these may be the same and some may be different. [Suggest items from your previously compiled list if the child does not come up with on her own.] *This is becoming a great list. Do you think we have everything?* [Wait for child to respond.]

4. Do the same thing, asking about different kinds of relationships (e.g., caregivers, teachers, mentors, therapists). Help the child to realise what aspects are important, regardless of the type of relationship, and what might be unique.

5. After completing a comprehensive list, go through each item and discuss whether it is a relative strength or an area for improvement. Elicit specific examples from the child's current and past relationships. The exercise is designed to familiarise the child to key components of relationship building and to identify personal barriers to making or maintaining social supports. It also emphasises the value of having social supports and that these are mutually beneficial.

    Okay, now let's take each of the things on the list and talk about whether you think it is something you are particularly good at or whether it is something that you could improve on. Everyone is not perfect at everything – we all could improve on certain things.

After the session

1. Take note of the child's general understanding of the material and whether social competency is a relative strength or weakness for the child.

2. Consider ways of building the child's self-competency if it is a weakness. Discuss this with the child's caregiver.

DEVELOPING A HEALTHY VIEW OF SELF

Goals

- To increase the child's awareness of her positive and negative views of self.
- To recognise the importance of balancing both positive and negative views of self.

Procedure

1. Explain the value of nurturing a positive view of self.

   People who have experienced trauma sometimes develop a more negative view of self. They may still view themselves in a good way, sometimes, but their negative view of self may take over. They may blame themselves for things that aren't their fault. They may focus on all of the times they failed at something. They may stop paying attention to times when they actually do a good job or when they succeed.

2. Explain why it is important to have a balanced sense of self that includes both positive and negative views.

   It is important to be aware of both positive and negative aspects of self. If one becomes more powerful than the other, we may lose sight of what we need to do to meet our goals and to live a healthy lifestyle. What do you think would happen, for instance, if someone's positive view of self overpowered [his/her] negative view of self? [Allow child to respond and discuss.] How about if that person's negative view of self overpowered [his/her] positive view of self? [Allow child to respond and discuss.]

3. Explore the child's healthy view of self by posing the following questions either in the context of a conversation or an activity or art project.

   What does your positive view of self look like?

   What does your negative view of self look like?

   How does your negative view of self challenge you to grow?

   Do other people see your positive view of self?

   Do other people see your negative view of self?

Creative applications

- Engage the child in making a self-portrait that reflects the child's positive and negative views of self. It could involve two portraits, one of the *negative view* and one of the *positive view*.

HEALTHY OPTIONS FOR COPING WITH STRESS

Goal

- To explore the child's use of healthy and unhealthy strategies for coping with stress.

Procedure

1. Discuss the difference between healthy and unhealthy types of coping.

   There are a lot of ways that we can respond to stress in our life. When we are able to tolerate stress or make it go away we call this coping with it. Some coping strategies are better than others. Can you think of any healthy coping strategies? [Allow child to respond.] How about unhealthy ones? [Allow child to respond.]

   Sometimes the unhealthy coping strategies work in reducing stress in the short term but actually make things worse for us in the long term. Can you think of any examples of how that could happen? [Allow child to respond.] That's right. Someone might choose to drink a lot of alcohol because she feels stressed out. The alcohol's effect on her brain might make her forget about the stress for a little while, but it doesn't solve the problem that caused the stress – and it is likely to make her feel worse later on. It could also create more problems for her. These unhealthy types of coping are sometimes called avoidance-focused strategies because the person is running away from the stress and the problem and often putting themselves in worse situations.

2. Discuss types of unhealthy coping strategies and explore whether the child has ever used any of these strategies to deal with stress. Encourage the child to come up with specific examples.

   Denying the problem or situation exists.

   Withdrawing or disengaging from the situation.

   Drinking alcohol or using substances to escape the situation.

   Engaging in risky behaviour to get one's mind off the situation.

   Becoming aggressive or destructive to oneself or others.

3. Discuss types of healthy coping strategies and explore whether the child has ever used any of these strategies to deal with stress. Again, encourage the child to come up with specific examples.

   Reinterpreting the situation.

   Learning from the situation.

   Asking other people to help you do something to fix the problem or situation.

   Asking other people for emotional support.

   Using humour to relieve some of the stress from the situation.

   Accepting the situation as a problem and setting a goal to solve it.

   Making a plan to change the situation.

   Using religion to cope with the situation.

CHAPTER 6
What is Trauma and How Does it Affect Us?

Explaining trauma on a continuum, from low-level daily stress to extreme forms of stress, can help children and their caregivers to better understand traumatic stress. The human brain has evolved with the ability to detect and process threat in the environment. Low-level stressors activate areas of the brain that help to manage positive and negative emotions, think through problems and make decisions. When a stressor is detected, the *emotional* brain sends signals to parts of the brain that communicate to other bodily systems that *something is wrong and needs attention*. The brain and body's response to the stressor is influenced by the degree of threat imposed. This is because the nervous system is working to find the appropriate balance between accelerating and enabling the *fight or flight* response or slowing down.

If the stressor is evaluated as low-level, the brain turns on other areas that help the person to remain calm, focused, and to think clearly. This enables the person to compare his current situation to memories of past situations and to come up with an effective strategy for overcoming the stressor. If the stressor is severe, however, the nervous system reacts by optimising the body's ability to survive. For example, blood is diverted from systems that are not imminently necessary, such as the digestive system, to the limbs, which are critical for escape and defence. The person does not have to think about it. The brain and body go on *autopilot*.

When stress is extreme or potentially traumatic, the brain's signal that *something is wrong* overwhelms areas of the brain equipped with organising and processing information. These areas do not come back online until after the person has already responded to the emergency. This is actually adaptive in truly imminent situations because cognitively processing information is too slow to promote survival. For example, if you suddenly come across a wild and dangerous animal, your brain does not need to think too hard about what to do – it just needs to tell you to get to a safe place. Sometimes during an emergency, people will act so quickly to protect themselves that they will not even remember what they did.

For a variety of reasons, some people are better equipped to turn down the brain's danger signal and return to a *resting state* or homeostasis after the threat is gone. Symptoms of traumatic stress are characteristic of a stress response system that is dysregulated or non-calibrated.

These individuals may have brains that have become more biased towards perceiving threat in the environment. Symptoms of PTSD and trauma-related psychopathology are best understood in the context of a dysregulated stress response system (Greene, Grasso and Ford, in press). Part of the goal of psychoeducation is to make these connections for the child and his caregiver. This enables them to begin to conceptualise how the child's reactive emotions, thoughts and behaviours may have emerged from processes linked to the stress response. In addition, it provides a rationale and context for the child's symptoms. In turn, the child and caregiver gain some control over the symptoms, which are no longer mystifying and intangible.

The following exercises are designed to educate the child and caregiver about trauma and its physical and emotional consequences and the development of trauma-related symptoms.

WHAT CAN BE TRAUMATIC?

Goals

- To educate the child on what types of events can be traumatic.
- To describe how trauma is defined.

Procedures

1. Refer to the 'What Kinds of Things Can Be Traumatic?' handout.

2. Describe the criteria used to define a trauma.

   There are a lot of things that could be traumatic. Sometimes an event can be traumatic for one person, but not traumatic for another person. It partly depends on people's perceptions of what happened. Possible traumatic experiences include someone dying, you or someone else coming close to dying, you or someone else being seriously hurt or injured, coming close to being seriously hurt or injured, and being sexually assaulted or coming close to being sexually assaulted. It is common for people to have at least one possible trauma happen to them in their lifetime. Do you know anyone else who had something happen that could be traumatic?

3. Discuss different types of potential trauma.

   Let's talk about some different kinds of possible trauma. There is a list on the handout. [Go down the list and explore whether the child has had any experience with these.]

4. Explain the relationship between traumatic stress and an exaggerated stress response system.

   Potential traumas are extreme stressors in our environment that activate the full extent of our stress response system. The stress response system is like our emergency response or alarm system. It is actually a good thing because it helps us to survive when we are in real danger. The problem is, some people have a hard time turning off the alarm system after the danger is gone – and they get stuck in this mode. Being stuck in survival mode makes it hard to do the things we're used to doing when we aren't in serious danger, such as schoolwork or listening to the teacher.

5. Explain why only some people develop traumatic stress after potential trauma.

   Not everyone develops traumatic stress after trauma. We don't really have a good answer as to why some people develop problems and other people don't. We think it may have to do with differences in people's genes, as well as other life experiences. The good news is that there are good approaches for reducing traumatic stress in people who develop it.

6. If the child's trauma is sexual abuse, provide additional information using the handout 'Sexual Abuse'. This defines sexual abuse and addresses some questions about sexual abuse.

7. If the child's trauma is associated with a traumatic loss, use the handout 'What is Traumatic Grief?' to facilitate a discussion about the difficulties of losing someone in the context of unexpected violence or trauma.

TEACHING THE STRESS RESPONSE

Goals

- To teach the child how the brain and body respond to non-extreme stress.
- To teach the child how the brain and body respond to extreme stress.
- To link the stress response to symptoms of post-traumatic stress.

Procedure

1. Study the illustrated steps depicted in Figure 6.1. These correspond to subsequent steps. The purpose of these is to provide you with a guide for how to teach the stress response to the child (and caregiver). You can do this in real time or you can use the illustrations provided and cut and paste them onto separate index cards or sheets of paper.

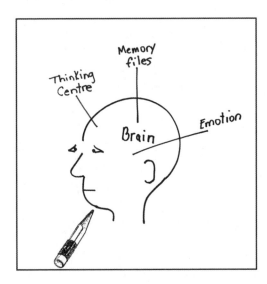 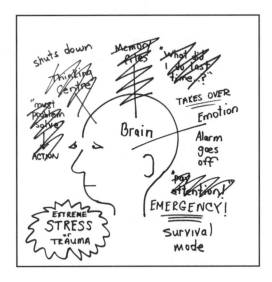

Step 1

Draw and label a diagram to represent the brain and three broad areas of the brain associated with the stress response. You can also draw a small figure to represent the peripheral nervous system.

Step 2

Modify the drawing to help explain the brain's response to a normal, everyday stressor. The 'emotion centre' sounds an alarm and signals the 'thinking centre' to pay attention. The 'memory centre' looks back into memory files to determine what one has done in past similar situations and informs the 'thinking centre'. The 'thinking centre' problem solves and makes and executes an action plan.

FIGURE 6.1 DRAW AND LABEL A DIAGRAM TO TEACH THE NORMAL STRESS RESPONSE

2. Explain the three goals of the exercise. Start with teaching the normal stress response. Provide several examples and ask the child to think of examples from his own life.

    Today I want to talk about how the brain and body respond to different types of stressors. There are some stressors that we experience every day – such as missing the bus or doing something embarrassing in public. What are some everyday things that might be stressful or upsetting to you? [Wait for child to respond.] *Good. And for the most part, we find ways of dealing with these smaller forms of stress.* [Explain the normal stress response using the steps in Figure 6.1.]

3. Next, explain the brain and body's response to extreme stress. Refer to Figure 6.2, or use your own visual aid.

    Then there are more extreme forms of stress or stress we might call trauma. Like other animals, we have evolved over time to respond to extreme stress in ways that help us to survive. Imagine walking on safari and coming across a very large and angry lion. How do you think you would respond? [Wait for child's response.] *Right. You would try to outrun the lion, climb a tree, fight back – anything that would help to defend you from being the lion's lunch. To do these things, we need all the energy that our body can possibly spare. It wouldn't make sense for the body to spend some energy on running away and some energy digesting food, for example. Instead, we have learned to stop the digestive system temporarily and to redirect the energy needed to do this to defending ourselves or running away. In addition, our brain turns down the area that is involved in thinking and reasoning. Think about it – if we had to think too much about what to do when coming across a lion, we would not respond quick enough and would have no chance. So, survival relies on our ability to react automatically, without having to think about it. All of this is our body's way of prioritising what needs to happen. And in these situations, survival is more important than digesting food.*

    Now, it's unlikely that we will come across a lion in this part of the world; however, there are a number of other extreme stressors that can bring about these responses. Can you think of any? [Wait for child's response.] *Absolutely. In fact, your brain and body surely has had an extreme stress response, and probably multiple times* [if the child has been exposed to chronic or multiple types of trauma]. [The following can be considered low-level therapeutic exposure in that it asks the child to recall how his body responded to the extreme stress.] *How did your brain and body respond to [child's trauma]? What bodily responses signalled that something was wrong or that you were in danger?*

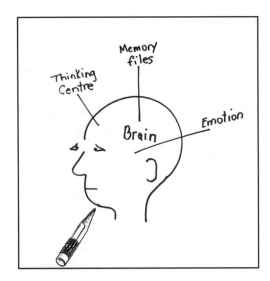

Step 1

Re-draw the brain and three broad areas of the brain.

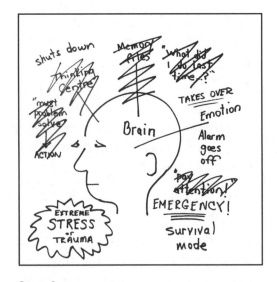

Step 2

Modify the drawing to help explain the brain's response to extreme stress or trauma. The 'emotion centre' activates an alarm that signals an emergency. It goes into survival mode. The 'emotion centre' turns down or deactivates parts of the 'thinking centre' and 'memory centre'. The brain and body are on 'autopilot' and the fight/flight response is implemented.

FIGURE 6.2 DRAW AND LABEL A DIAGRAM TO TEACH THE EXTREME STRESS RESPONSE

4.   Once you feel the child has grasped these concepts, move on to explaining how extreme stress responses and subsequent dysregulation of the stress response system is associated with the development of symptoms of traumatic stress. Refer to Figure 6.3.

Now I want us to take a look at the different types of symptoms or problems associated with traumatic stress. Remember that we said the stress response is adaptive or helpful when we are in a dangerous or threatening situation – however, some people's brains and bodies continue to respond to extreme stress even after the danger or threat is gone. When this happens, the body is still prioritising survival over other things such as digestion and thinking and reasoning. Some people call it being in survival mode. Imagine how hard it would be to pay attention in class if your brain is turning down the area that helps you think and reason – it would be pretty hard. So, being in survival mode is not adaptive or helpful in safe situations.

Being in survival mode also means that smaller, daily stressors may be treated as though they are more extreme stressors. Also, things that weren't stressors before the traumatic event may become stressors because they remind the person of the trauma. These could be as simple as the smell of someone's perfume or the way something looks. These things are all consistent with how we define post-traumatic stress disorder (PTSD). Let's look at and go over the different symptoms that are associated with PTSD.

Intrusion Symptoms

Having bad dreams or nightmares.

Bad memories pop into your head.

Feeling like it is happening again when it's not.

Having flashbacks.

Having bodily responses to reminders of the trauma.

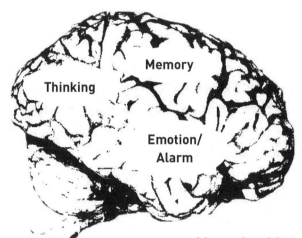

Avoidance

Trying to avoid thoughts and feelings that remind you of the trauma or how you felt during the trauma.

Trying to avoid people, places, activities or situations that remind you of the trauma.

Negative Mood and Cognitions

Expecting the worst about yourself, others and the world.

Blaming yourself for the cause or consequence of it.

Fear, horror, anger, guilt or shame.

Loss of interest in activities or things you used to like to do.

Feeling disconnected from others.

Trouble feeling positive emotions.

Arousal and Reactivity

Irritable or aggressive behaviour.

Reckless or risky behaviour.

Feeling on 'high-alert'.

Trouble concentrating.

Trouble falling or staying asleep.

FIGURE 6.3 STRESS RESPONSE AND PTSD SYMPTOMS

After the session

1. Take note of how well the child grasped these ideas. This information can be used to provide a rationale for treatment and to explain the therapeutic process.

CHAPTER 7
How Will Psychotherapy Help?

Once the child and caregiver have a good understanding of the stress response system and symptoms of traumatic stress, it is important to provide a rationale for the therapeutic techniques that will be used. If you are still unsure about what therapeutic model or components you will use with this child, you might use this time also to discuss options with the child and caregiver and to elicit feedback that may guide your decision making.

Although therapies with the strongest research evidence for treating anxiety problems, including post-traumatic stress, involve therapeutic exposure, some children will be quite resistant to it and may even refuse outright. These children are at high risk for treatment dropout. Keep in mind that there are different forms of therapeutic exposure, some that are less intensive than others. The child's resistance may help decide which of these you choose to use. Also, children should become less resistant over time, and so most therapies advise a gradual exposure approach. Where you start will depend on the child's level of resistance.

In addition, there may be situations in which therapeutic exposure may not be the most appropriate treatment modality – at least initially. Specifically, therapeutic exposure is less effective with individuals who have experienced chronic adversity and trauma, as well as co-occurring internalising and externalising behaviour problems and symptoms that are characterised by severe emotion dysregulation (Harvey and Taylor 2010). Thus, some children may respond best to therapy if emotion regulation problems are directly addressed. There is some evidence that emotion regulation training enhances the effectiveness of therapeutic exposure through acceptance, tolerance and active modification of negative emotions (Cloitre *et al.* 2010). Indeed, with children seeking to work through trauma memories therapeutically, building competence in emotion regulation is often recommended as a first step.

The following exercise provides a structure for explaining to the child how treatment works.

EXPLAINING HOW TREATMENT WORKS

Goals

- To provide the child and caregiver with evidence of treatment benefit.

- To teach the child and caregiver the treatment protocol.

- To explain to the child and caregiver the theoretical rationale behind the therapeutic approach.

Procedure

1. Use your case conceptualisation to narrow down your list of potential treatment options. Be prepared to answer questions about these treatments and to explain the rationale behind these approaches in a way that will be understood by the child and caregiver.

   Briefly review the stress response system and its association with post-traumatic stress symptoms. Ask the child what she thinks can be done to reset the stress response system and to reduce symptoms.

   Can you remember what the primary symptoms of PTSD are? [Wait for response.] Good. I want to talk about how we might go about improving these problems. Knowing what you know now about the stress response and how it can get stuck in survival mode, how do you think we can change it? [Explore the child's ideas.] Those are some good ideas.

2. Explain what habituation is and how it involves retraining the stress response system.

   We want to reset or recalibrate the stress response system. Actually, I like to think about it as retraining the stress response system. We need to get the nervous system to realise that it is not in danger and need not be operating in survival mode. We cannot simply tell it to do this, no more than we can train a dog to roll over by talking to him. There are some things our bodies do that happen automatically – such as breathing or sweating. We can't just tell these things to stop.

   One of the things we do is 'prove' to the nervous system that it is safe. Imagine you get a new pet and that the pet is initially frightened of you. You are a stranger and much bigger than it. Over time, though, you care for it and show it that you aren't threatening or dangerous. Even though the pet is nervous initially, the pet learns that there is no need to be nervous. Instead of threatening the pet, you actually make it feel loved. In a similar way, your nervous system may be upset when exposed to something that reminds it of the trauma, but over time it will start to realise that despite being exposed to the reminder, it is safe. The reminder could be a person or a place that is associated with the trauma, or it could be the memory of the trauma itself. This process of the nervous system learning not to be upset by a trauma reminder or the trauma memory is called habituation. [Use Figure 7.1 to illustrate.]

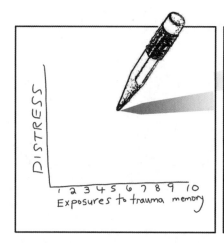 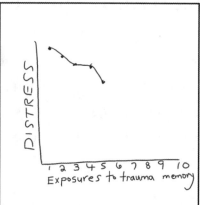 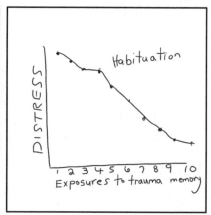

Step 1

Draw a chart with an x- and y-axis. Put 'Distress' on the y-axis and put 'Exposures to trauma memory' on the x-axis.

Step 2

Plot the first few points along on the chart, explaining that initially the person is highly distressed when exposed to the trauma memory and that this starts to go down pretty quickly.

Step 3

Plot the remaining time points and explain that habituation involves reduced distress between the different exposures.

FIGURE 7.1 DRAW AND LABEL A DIAGRAM TO EXPLAIN HABITUATION

3. Explain the notion behind emotional and cognitive processing of the trauma memory. You want the child to come away with the idea that she should strive to (a) gain more control of the trauma memory, (b) better understand how the trauma has influenced her life, and (c) reorganise the trauma memory so that it is less threatening and overwhelming.

   The other thing we want to do is to help the brain to better understand what happened and to gain a sense of control over it. Because people who experience trauma often want to get away from the memory and avoid it, the information from the trauma is usually disorganised and in pieces. This actually makes it more scary and less in control.

   Think about your locker at school. Imagine that whenever you put something into your locker you just opened it up and threw it in. Over time, your locker would become a mess. There wouldn't be room to put new things in it and you wouldn't be able to find anything in it. Your locker wouldn't be very functional any more. Instead, imagine it becoming so full of things that you didn't know what to do with that every now and then it just pops open and all that stuff just falls out for everyone to see.

   This is sort of like throwing information about the trauma into the locker and letting it get so disorganised and full of stuff that you lose control over it. In therapy what we try to do is to pull everything out of that locker and sort it. We put the stuff into small piles and neatly organise it. Then we put it back so that you can close the locker without it opening up on its own, you understand what is in there and how it is organised – and you feel more in control of it. It is a way for the brain to learn to use new information to better deal with the trauma memory. [See Figure 7.2 for an example of how to explain new learning.]

4. Introduce the different ways of accomplishing habituation and trauma memory processing. If you have already narrowed down the treatment options for the child, only discuss those options.

There are different ways of training your nervous system to habituate and for reorganising the trauma information. It is our job to find out which approach will work best for you. What do you think of all of this so far? [Wait for response.] *One of the ways we can do this is by doing something called Imaginal Exposure. This is where I would ask you to sit comfortably in this room and tell about what happened as though it were currently happening. For example, if I were telling about what happened this morning I would say, 'I am walking out of the house and using my keys to unlock the car doors. I slowly get into the car and pull the door shut. I start the car and the radio blares.' You would do this from start to finish for up to 45 minutes. If you finished before the time was up, you would simply start again. The purpose of this is to show your nervous system that you can face the trauma memory and still be safe.* [Pause.] *Another way to do this is by writing out what happened – still telling about it as though it were currently happening. You could write it yourself or you could dictate to me as I type. You would rewrite the narrative a number of times – each time adding more detail to it.* [You may feel that given the child's cognitive skills, she is better off developing a narrative comprised of pictures.]

Step 1

Draw a picture that represents an analogy between the strong brain connections to maladaptive or symptomatic behaviour in the presence of trauma reminders. Explain that the brain has become accustomed to responding to trauma reminders by becoming avoidant or engaging in unhealthy coping techniques and that it is like a 'super highway'; it has developed such that the maladaptive response is the fastest and most likely response. Explain that we want to 'teach' the brain 'new information' that will create a connection between the brain and healthy coping techniques in the presence of trauma reminders. In this depiction, healthy coping and unhealthy coping (avoidance) are represented as islands.

FIGURE 7.2 EXPLAIN HOW NEW LEARNING ESTABLISHES NEW CONNECTIONS IN THE BRAIN ASSOCIATED WITH HEALTHY COPING AND WEAKENS OLD CONNECTIONS ASSOCIATED WITH UNHEALTHY COPING

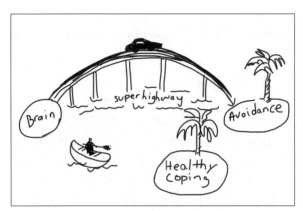

Step 2

Explain that initially we want to establish a small connection to healthy coping behaviours – like sending out a boat. The connection may not always be made and it may be slow, but it will happen some of the time.

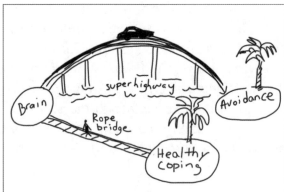

Step 3

Over time, the connection will become stronger and perhaps a more permanent connection will be made – like a rope bridge between the brain and healthy coping. This will speed up the connection and allow for more 'traffic'.

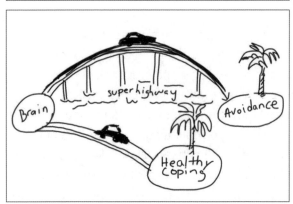

Step 4

With more usage of the rope bridge there will be a need to establish a stronger and even more permanent bridge that can accommodate cars – perhaps a one-lane road. This happens because the brain is becoming more used to responding to trauma reminders with healthy coping behaviour.

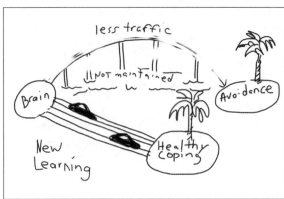

Step 5

Over time the one-lane road becomes a multi-lane highway that can accommodate more traffic and can make the connection between the brain and healthy coping much quicker. Also, because the old 'super highway' between the brain and unhealthy behaviour is not being used as much, it starts to fall apart or become weaker. It is less well maintained. So, even though the connection does not go away altogether, it becomes very weak. Thus, this 'new learning' makes for new, stronger connections in the brain.

FIGURE 7.2 CONTINUED

5. Gauge the child's level of resistance to undergoing exposure to the trauma memory.

   What do you think of this so far? [Wait for child's response.] *What questions do you have about this process?* [Wait for child's response and explore any fears the child conveys.]

6. Explain that the process is gradual and reinforce the child's perception that she will be able to handle exposure therapy.

   We are going to take a gradual approach. By this I mean that I will not ask you to do everything at once. If you were training to run a marathon, you probably wouldn't run the entire marathon at your first practice. You would work up to it. By working up to it you are getting better and better each time until you can run the marathon. That is what training is all about.

After the session

1. Take note of the child's level of resistance to therapeutic exposure and trauma memory processing. Although the child's resistance should decrease as sessions progress, it will also vary depending on other life events and stressors in the child's life. It will also be influenced by your therapeutic rapport with the child, which is also a moving target. It is likely that you will need to revisit the child's resistance along the way, reminding her that it is common to be avoidant of the trauma memory, but that progress and success in treatment requires pushing through this resistance. Continue to encourage the child through this. You may also engage the caregiver in encouraging the child and praising her for doing exposure work. Exposure therapy can be highly uncomfortable. With the right 'dosage' and subsequent reward (e.g., praise), the child will tolerate the therapy and gain a sense of confidence and achievement afterwards.

CHAPTER 8

Regulating Intense Emotion from the Bottom Up

Teaching the child to develop his ability to regulate bodily reactions to stress can help him to better cope with stress on a day-to-day basis, as well as tolerate therapeutic exposure and processing of the traumatic memory. Bodily reactions can be frightening and overwhelming. If children learn to temper these reactions and exert some control over them using breathing or other relaxation techniques, then these reactions become less obstructive. Commonly taught exercises include abdominal breathing, muscle tension relaxation and mindfulness techniques. The goal is for the child to establish a menu of options that he can draw on in stressful situations.

The following exercises can be used to help the child to develop and improve these skills. These are common ingredients of many therapies, and so it is worth exploring whether the child has ever learned them before. In addition, the child may already have positive strategies for managing his physiological reactions to stress, and these should be recognised and reinforced.

LEARNING HOW TO BREATHE

Goals

- To teach abdominal breathing as a means to relax the body.
- To emphasise that physiological relaxation (i.e., from the bottom up) can reduce negative emotion and anxiety.
- To encourage the child to practise abdominal breathing outside of therapy.

Procedure

1. Introduce the objectives of this exercise. Explain the influence the body has on our emotional system. Explain that we can use techniques to modify our physiological state in order to reduce stress and anxiety. Explore whether the child has used or currently uses these strategies.

   Today I want to focus on ways of using our bodies to cope with stress and to improve the way we feel. We have all done this before. I want to talk about specific techniques that you can use at home or at school – techniques that you can easily carry with you anywhere. Remember back to our discussion of the stress response system. Can you remember how the body responds to stress? [Wait for child to respond.] Exactly. Our muscles tighten. Our heart rate increases. We sweat. Our bodies get jittery. Our breath gets faster and shorter. All of these things.

   Now, what if we were to do the opposite of these things or do things that would reduce the heart rate, sweating and muscle tension? Do you think we can reverse the emotional stress we feel? [Pause.] I think so. That is the goal.

2. Introduce and explain abdominal breathing. Engage the child in three minutes of abdominal breathing.

   The first technique I want to talk to you about is called abdominal breathing. Now, you might think that is silly – as we're constantly breathing – but normally how we breathe is influenced by our emotions. Abdominal breathing is like taking control of the way we breathe in order to change our emotional state. So, instead of breathing fast and short, abdominal breathing is deliberately breathing slow and deep. Let's take a few seconds to take some quick and short breaths. Take note on how it feels. Ready, go. [Let several seconds pass.] Good. So, that's what happens when we are under stress.

   Now, I want us to try some slow deep breaths – and this time, when you breathe in or inhale, do it so that your stomach rises. [Demonstrate.] You will know that you are doing this right if you put your hand on your stomach and you feel your stomach rise. Let's try a few of these. Follow my lead. Ready, inhale. [Inhale with your hand on your stomach.] Exhale. [Exhale slowly with your hand on your stomach and repeat.] How does that feel? [Wait for child's response.] Now, let's do this for a whole three minutes. You might try closing your eyes while you do it. [Be aware that for some children, closing their eyes makes them feel vulnerable and increases their stress level.] How was that for you?

[Wait for child to respond.] *It takes some getting used to. It is common for people to feel like it is not working in the beginning and to become frustrated. I tell them to stick with it because it will get easier with practice. Sure enough, when they stop trying so hard to do it right and just let their bodies adjust to it naturally, they really like it.*

MUSCLE-TENSION RELAXATION AND THE BODY SCAN

Goals

- To teach muscle tension relaxation as a means of relaxing the body.
- To encourage the child to practise muscle tension relaxation outside of therapy.

Procedure

1. Introduce and explain muscle tension relaxation.

    Muscle tension relaxation sounds complicated but it's really not. Did you ever do that trick where you stand with your arm against the wall and you push your arm into the wall as hard as you can for up to a minute so that when you release it, it seems like your arm just floats up? [Wait for response.] *Let's try it.* [Have the child stand flush against the wall and instruct him to press his arm against the wall as hard as possible for 15 seconds.] *Now step away from the wall. How does your arm feel?* [Wait for response.] *When you max out your muscles by tensing them, then relax them, they actually become more relaxed than they were before you started. Muscle tension relaxation is simply going through your body and tensing and releasing your muscles.*

    One way to do it is to start at your toes and move your way up. Do you want to try it? Okay, you can close your eyes if you'd like. Start by squeezing or clenching your toes. Squeeze as hard as you can. I'll tell you when to release. [Wait ten seconds.] *Okay, release. Feel the energy flow out of them when you let go. Now squeeze your calves. Tight. Hold them there.* [Wait ten seconds.] *Good, release. Now your knees, thighs and hamstrings. Squeeze hard. Good. Hold it.* [Wait ten seconds.] *Okay, release. Now your buttocks. Hold it.* [Ten seconds.] *Release. Now tighten your stomach muscles. Good.* [Ten seconds.] *Release. Move to your chest and upper back. Hold it.* [Ten seconds.] *Release. Now tighten your neck and jaw muscles.* [Ten seconds.] *Good, release. Now tense all of your face muscles – your cheeks, forehead, ears – good, hold it.* [Ten seconds.] *Now let go. Move to your biceps and triceps – the inner and outer part of your arms. Hold them tight.* [Ten seconds.] *Now let go. Now tighten your forearms and clench your fists. Really tight. Good.* [Ten seconds.] *Now let go. Now, tighten up your entire body, all of your muscles, as much as you can. Hold it for ten seconds.* [Ten seconds.] *Good, now when you let go this time feel all of the energy flow out of your body, leaving you with a body that is fully relaxed and calm.*

2. Introduce and practise the 'body scan'.

    Another technique you can use that does not involve tensing and releasing your muscles is what we call the body scan. Like muscle tension relaxation, we go through our body, starting at the toes. The purpose of this, however, is to pay attention to all of the small parts of your body and willingly to relax those areas. Sometimes there are parts of our body that are stressed and tense and we don't even know it. The body scan helps to identify those areas that are particularly tense, and to loosen them up.

I like to imagine that the part of my body that I am concentrating on is glowing and that this 'glow' is moving up through my body. As it moves through different areas, those areas are relaxed. Let's try it. Close your eyes if you'd like. Start at your toes. Imagine that they are glowing. Now imagine that 'glow' start to move up slowly from your toes to your feet. As it moves, you feel the tenseness leave your toes and feet. Let it move up from your toes to your shins and calves. Imagine that the glow is making them tingle. Now let the glow move from your calves to your knees and thighs. Let it sit there for a few seconds. Imagine that the glow is relaxing these muscles. [Pause.] Now it moves from your thighs to your buttocks and waist. These areas are relaxed. Now it moves to your stomach. Feel your stomach muscles loosen and your stomach let go. Now it moves up to your chest. Imagine your chest glowing. [Pause.] Now let it move to your neck, then your face and head. They are all glowing and becoming relaxed. Now it slips into your arms and you feel your biceps and triceps let go. Then it moves into your hands and fingertips. Feel the tingle. Now all of your body is completely relaxed and the glow slips out from your fingers. Take a deep breath and feel how relaxed your body is.

THE PERKS OF PHYSICAL ACTIVITY

Goals

- To explain the benefits of physical activity on dealing with stress.
- To encourage the child to engage in regular physical activity.

Procedures

1. Explain how physical activity can relax the body.

   Another way to help your body to relax is by engaging it in physical activity. Physical activity provides all sorts of health benefits. First, it decreases what we call stress hormones in the body. Stress hormones are special chemicals in the body linked to the stress response system we talked about. Physical activity also increases chemicals in our body that make it feel good – such as endorphins. Endorphins also boost your mood. As a whole, regular physical activity can reduce your body's physiological reactivity to everyday stress. Finally, regular physical activity or exercise is essential for good health. When you are healthy, your body is in a better place to cope with stressors. Poor health can actually cause stress. Think about it – poor health makes you more vulnerable to viruses and other illnesses and can really slow you down.

2. Explore with the child what kinds of physical activity he likes to engage in – or could engage in. Make a list of these activities.

   What kinds of things do you do that are physical? [If the child cannot generate any activities help him to brainstorm some possibilities and encourage him to try to engage in them before the next session.]

THE STRESS SOLUTION CARD

Goals

- To encourage the child to use relaxation strategies outside of therapy.
- To provide the child with a portable aid for accessing the menu of relaxation options.

Procedure

1. Summarise the relaxation techniques learned to date (e.g., abdominal breathing, muscle tension relaxation, body scan, physical activity). Discuss strategies for using these techniques outside of therapy.

2. Develop a 'Stress Solution Card', a pocket-sized card that outlines a personalised set of strategies for the child to refer to (see Figure 8.1). The cognitive coping techniques discussed in the next chapter can be incorporated on this card.

   So we talked about a number of different techniques for relaxing the body. Which one do you think is most effective for you? [Wait for response.] When do you see yourself using these? [Wait for response.] It is important that these are practised pretty regularly so that they will work best when you actually need them to. So, I recommend that you practise these when you are not stressed. This way, when you are under stress and use one or more of these techniques, you will get the most benefit from them. This is also true of the other strategies we'll be talking about in the next session.

My Stress Solution Card

Focus on my body

Remember to breathe deep into the belly

Do a body scan

Tense and release my muscles

Go skateboarding

Focus on my thoughts

One problem at a time

Tell myself to calm down

Is this really a problem or does it only seem like a problem?

FIGURE 8.1 THE STRESS SOLUTION CARD

CHAPTER 9

Regulating Intense Emotion from the Top Down

Like physiological techniques to regulate intense emotion, cognitive techniques help children to better cope with everyday stress, as well as to tolerate thinking and talking about the traumatic event in session. Cognitive techniques work from the top down or from the *inside out* (i.e., the brain to the body). Here the brain is messaging the body to change its physical state. In reality, the processes are more dynamic than that – but it is a helpful way of thinking about it. Cognitive techniques include things such as *self-talk*, identifying and falsifying unhelpful thoughts and paying attention to thoughts triggered by trauma-related stimuli.

Like the previous chapter, the goal here is for the child to establish a menu of options on which she can draw in stressful situations. The following techniques can be used to help the child to develop and improve these skills. These are common ingredients of many therapies, and so it is worth exploring whether the child has ever learned these before. In addition, the child may already have positive strategies for managing her physiological reactions to stress, and these should be recognised and reinforced. You may choose to introduce these techniques in the same session or across different sessions depending on how much you want to emphasise each, as well as how much guidance the child requires.

COGNITIVE COPING: PUTTING OUR BRAIN TO GOOD USE

Goals

- To teach cognitive methods of coping with stress.
- To explain that cognitive techniques (i.e., from the top down) can reduce negative emotion, anxiety and bodily reactions to stress.

Procedure

1. Explain the influence that our thoughts have on our emotions and how our body responds to stress.

   Today I want to focus on ways of using our thoughts to help to cope with stress, relax the body and improve our mood. I am going to talk about a number of techniques. My hope is that we will find some to be particularly helpful to you. You might actually use some of these already. [Explain how thoughts, emotions and behaviours are interconnected.] I want to start by talking about the brain and body again. Remember that part of our brain deals mainly with thinking things through and making decisions. [Point to where the prefrontal cortex is located.] This is the front part of the brain, right about here. This part of the brain is what makes humans unique from most other animals. It gives us the ability to think about ourselves in ways that other animals cannot. For example, humans can think about how they think. We don't think other animals can quite do that. People have called this metacognition. Because we have this ability, we have more control over how we perceive the things around us and how we respond to them. What goes on in our prefrontal cortex – our thinking about and interpreting ourselves and the things around us – has a direct influence on our emotions and our behaviours.

   For example, imagine we see a snake in the garden. The part of our brain that deals with emotion suddenly lights up and we feel surprised and maybe fear. When the thinking part of our brain realises that it is not a snake but a part of the garden hose, it sends a message to our emotion centre to turn down or shut off the fear. Without the connection between the thinking part of the brain and the emotion centre, we wouldn't have this ability – we would just react.

   Here is another example. Let's say you had plans to go out with a friend and the friend never showed up. At first you are upset and angry that the friend forgot about you or didn't think it was important enough to follow through with the original plans. [Pause.] But there is another way to interpret this situation. You remember that your friend has a relative who is very sick in hospital. You also remember that your friend has never done this to you before. Instead of thinking that your friend has wronged you, you realise that your friend may have had to change her plans at the last minute because of something unexpected – perhaps related to the relative in hospital. Still, another way to interpret this is that your friend simply forgot and didn't mean to wrong you. So our prefrontal cortex or thinking brain allows us to interpret situations in a variety of ways.

2. Explain that people who have experienced trauma can be more likely to interpret a situation as threatening or more negative.

Different interpretations can lead to very different feelings and behaviours.

It turns out that people often make mistakes in interpreting situations – interpreting things in ways that make them feel upset or stressed. Some people do this more than others. It also turns out that people who have experienced extreme stress or trauma tend to interpret things as being more threatening, dangerous or negative than others. These people have to learn how to recognise that they may be interpreting a situation as more negative than it is and to reinterpret situations. Does this ever happen to you where you initially think something is worse than it really is? [Allow child to comment.]

3. Explain that we can use techniques to modify the way we think about things in order to reduce stress and anxiety.

What is important here is that our brain makes mistakes. Our job is to catch those mistakes or those exaggerations. What do you think are some ways we can use our thinking brain to reinterpret situations and effectively cope with stress? [Allow child to respond and engage in discussion.]

Creative applications

- Give the child a demonstration of the fallibility of the brain. There are several optical illusions that you can use. A favourite presentation is the 'Invisible Gorilla' by Dr Daniel Simons and colleagues. It demonstrates our selective attention. The film clip features two teams that are passing a number of basketballs to each other – a white-shirt team and a black-shirt team. The viewer is instructed to count the number of passes made by the white-shirt team. As the viewer does this, entering from the right is a person dressed in a full gorilla suit. The gorilla walks to the centre of the screen and pounds its chest before walking out on the left side of the screen. The majority of viewers later claim that they did not notice the gorilla. This is viewable at www.theinvisiblegorilla.com/videos.html. The site also has other illusions to choose from.

REACTIVE VS. PROACTIVE THOUGHTS

Goals

- To teach the difference between automatic or reactive thoughts and processed or proactive thoughts.
- To encourage the child to identify reactive thoughts and to work towards generating proactive thoughts.

Procedure

1. Explain the difference between reactive and proactive thoughts. Use Table 9.1 to refer to examples. Encourage the child to come up with other examples. Also encourage the child to think of specific times when she had reactive and proactive thoughts.

    I want to talk about the difference between two different kinds of thoughts we have: reactive and proactive thoughts. A while ago we talked about the stress response system and how the body goes into survival mode when it is in extreme stress or in a traumatic situation. When we come across a hungry lion, we don't have time to do a lot of thinking – we just have to react. When the body is in survival mode, our thoughts are reactive. Run! Get out of here! These are thoughts that are strongly influenced by the emotion centre of the brain. They are not thought through.

    We have reactive thoughts even when we aren't in extremely dangerous situations. Go back to the example I gave about your friend who did not follow through with your plans to get together. The reactive thought might have been, 'My friend doesn't care about me', or 'I guess I don't have good friends!' After thinking about it and processing the situation, however, we decide that there are other alternatives. Your friend could have had an emergency or might simply have forgotten about it. These other thoughts – the ones about other possibilities – are processed thoughts because the prefrontal cortex or thinking centre has spent more time and energy thinking the situation through. I call them proactive thoughts because they are thoughts that attempt to use more information to make sense of something and to gain control of it rather than simply responding to it.

    Reactive thoughts are kind of like rough and unfinished cars out of a factory. They don't have all of the components to make them fully functional. Proactive thoughts are like the finished products, after being refined and perfected – a car with all of its components. Let's think of some reactive thoughts. [After generating several reactive thoughts.] Now let's think of some proactive thoughts that might be used instead of the reactive thoughts.

TABLE 9.1 REACTIVE VS. PROACTIVE THOUGHTS

Reactive Thoughts	Proactive Thoughts
This is the worst situation ever.	This is challenging, but I've got through this before.
I am going to hurt you.	I am very angry right now and need some personal space.
People think I'm a big joke.	It is okay for me to laugh at myself once in a while.
I need this right now and I am going to take it.	This is something I would like, but I can be patient.
That's it – I've ruined everything.	Okay, I made a mistake and created a problem – but I will work on it.
My mother does not understand me at all.	My mother and I have a misunderstanding and we need to talk about this.

The key here is not to stop having reactive thoughts, but to realise when you have them and to generate proactive thoughts to go along with them. Reactive thoughts are important in truly threatening or dangerous situations. They tell us when something is wrong. Proactive thoughts help us to respond to situations using more of the available information. It is important to remind yourself to step back from situations to take a moment to help your brain to figure out what your stress response system is telling you and to realise what is happening. Next, gather information from the current situation and memories of past situations to make sense of what is going on. Using this information, make an informed decision or respond or behave in an informed way. Let's go through some possible scenarios.

Creative applications

- *Cartoon bubbles.* Compile a set of pictures and/or cartoons of people in various situations. You can get these from magazines, newspapers or comic strips. Cut out a number of cartoon thought bubbles from white paper. Have the child generate a thought statement for each scenario, write it on the cartoon bubble and glue or tape it to the picture. You can do the same type of thing with short video clips.

TALKING TO YOURSELF IS NOT CRAZY

Goals

- To explain that positive self-talk can be an effective way to reduce stress.
- To encourage the child to monitor her self-talk.

Procedure

1. Explain what self-talk is and how it can be used effectively to reduce stress.

   We all talk to ourselves. Maybe we don't do this so other people can hear it, but we all have an inner dialogue in our head. Do you agree? It is kind of like that book that many read as a child, 'The Little Engine that Could', where the train repeatedly says, 'I think I can…I think I can…I think I can…' It may seem silly, but we do this kind of talking to ourselves all the time. The thing is, sometimes what we say to ourselves is helpful and sometimes it is not all that helpful. In fact, some people put themselves down a lot in their heads by saying things like, 'I'm so stupid', or 'I wish I could be that good', or 'I give up!' This kind of negative self-talk is very unhelpful. The thing I want to talk to you about is recognising when you are using negative self-talk and to change it so that you are using positive self-talk. Instead of putting yourself down, you could say to yourself, 'Don't worry…you'll do better next time', or 'I don't have to be good at everything.' We can be our own best friend – or our worst enemy. Let's try it. Let's both close our eyes and use some positive self-talk. Just for a minute or two. Ready? [Wait for child to signal.] Okay, go. [Wait about a minute.] Okay, how did that feel? [Wait for child's response.] I use positive self-talk a lot. It is a good way of coping with stress. I tell myself to calm down, that the situation is not worth getting all worked up about.

2. Help the child make a list that she can keep as a reference. See Figure 9.1 for some suggestions.

   Let's make a list of things you could say to yourself in stressful situations.

What to Tell Myself when Under Stress

- This will pass – you can get through this.
- Take it one thing at a time.
- Slow down and step back for a minute.
- Give yourself a break; you're doing the best you can.
- People are on your side and ready to support you.
- You are strong and can handle this.
- Don't waste your energy stressing over this.
- It really isn't that bad.
- Take a deep breath.
- Remember to use your relaxation techniques.
- You need to go for a walk.
- Everything will be okay.
- There are people who can help you.
- You're a good person.

FIGURE 9.1 POSITIVE SELF-TALK

RUMINATING AND AVOIDING

Goals

- To teach the child about ruminating and avoiding.
- To encourage the child to identify when she is ruminating or avoiding and to switch tactics.

Procedure

1. Discuss the importance of recognising unhealthy cognitive tactics for dealing with stress so that they can be replaced with healthy strategies.

   There are two ways that people sometimes deal with stress that are unhealthy and tend to make us feel worse. One of these is called rumination. *The other is called* avoidance. *Both of these strategies use up a lot of our energy and wear us out. Although they may help to escape the stress in the short term, they do not solve the problem in the long term.*

2. Explain what rumination is.

   Rumination is kind of like getting into a clothes dryer. This is when we get stuck going over the same thoughts or the same scenario over and over and over again. Let me give you an example. Let's say that I was out in a fancy restaurant and that the dining room was very quiet, and that all of a sudden I trip and knock the waiter into another table so that all of the food and beverages he was carrying spilled all over the five people sitting there. This would make me pretty embarrassed and would probably spoil my dinner experience. Later, I would be ruminating if I went over and over what happened at the restaurant in my head – almost like reliving the embarrassment.

   This is similar to the symptom of post-traumatic stress where people go over and over the traumatic event in their minds and can't seem to get away from it. It turns out that people who have symptoms of post-traumatic stress are very good at ruminating. Do you ever find yourself doing this? [Allow child to respond.] Sometimes we do it without even realising it. So, how do we know when we are ruminating? Sometimes it is helpful to focus on a problem until we have figured it out. However, some things are outside of our control, and spinning or ruminating on the problem isn't going to get us anywhere. Instead, it just makes us feel the same distressing emotions over and over again. You might know that you are ruminating if you can't seem to get certain thoughts out of your head, or certain thoughts or events seem to go on and on in an endless loop, or if you seem to get stuck in strong negative feelings. People may have their own ways of recognising when they are ruminating. What do you think are some cues that you are ruminating? [Wait for child's response and continue to discuss as applicable.]

3. Explain what avoidance is.

   The other strategy, avoidance, is when we deliberately try to get away from the problem or negativity. We just want to shut it off. Avoiding is like shutting down, numbing out or withdrawing. A good example of this is sitting on the couch, endlessly flipping channels on the television, not really watching anything, but just flipping as a distraction from thinking about the problem. Another example is when people withdraw and block out what is going on around them. They sort of 'check out' and do not respond to anyone or anything. The problem with these strategies is that the more we try to avoid the problem or negative thoughts, the stronger they seem to come back to haunt us. And avoiding or shutting down does not solve the problem, so it is still there when we return.

Other forms of avoiding include eating large amounts of food, drinking alcohol, smoking marijuana or taking other drugs in order to escape feelings or thoughts. Have you ever done any avoiding or checking out to deal with negative feelings or stress? [Let child respond and discuss.] *So, how do we know when we are avoiding? Well, if we find ourselves spending a lot of time alone or away from other people, or deliberately trying to do things that distract us from thinking about the problem or negative thoughts, we might be actively avoiding. Some people actually feel it in their body in the form of tension or an upset stomach or headaches. What are some ways that you know you are starting to be avoidant?* [Wait for child to respond and discuss.]

4. Discuss a healthier approach to organising and approaching problems.

So, let's talk about some more healthy ways of managing stress. Stress is a normal part of life. Rather than becoming overwhelmed by stress and trying to avoid it or getting stuck in it, we can find ways that will allow us to take a break from it while still taking time to deal with whatever is causing the stress. There will always be problems that we have to deal with: a big report due at school or an argument with a parent. We can't attend to every problem at once. One suggestion is to schedule a time to think through certain problems or situations in order to work them out. By scheduling this time, you can free up other time to take a break from stress and focus on things you enjoy, being active, spending time with your friends or family, or just relaxing. This is very different from avoiding problems, because you set a time to problem solve.

Let's try something. I would like you to try to close your eyes and imagine that all of the worries and problems you've had this week are swirling around your head. What I want you to do is to imagine taking each of those things and putting them in a box. Then imagine that you mark a day and a time on the box for when you want to open it and think through the problems. Then close it up and put it aside. By doing this, these problems are no longer hanging over your head. They aren't forgotten about – but they are put away until a specific time when you will deal with them. Some people like to write the problems down in a journal or on a pad along with a date and time for when they intend to sit down and problem solve. What do you think would work for you? [Allow child to respond and discuss other possible tactics.]

MINDFULNESS

Goals

- To teach the child what mindfulness is.
- To encourage the child to practise being mindful on a daily basis.

Procedure

1. Introduce the notion of mindfulness and its relevance for reducing stress and promoting wellness.

    Mindfulness is a term that comes from Eastern medicine and Buddhist culture. It refers to being aware of ourselves and our surroundings, in the present. So often we are either caught up in the past or thinking about the future that we are not truly in the present. We lose touch with where we are, what we are doing and what is going on around us. Can you think of a situation where you just followed your typical routine, such as brushing your teeth and getting ready for school, and got somewhere without really knowing how you got there? [Allow child to respond.] Being mindful is about paying attention to the entire process and taking yourself out of autopilot mode.

    Being mindful is the opposite of avoiding and ruminating. It is the practice of focusing on the present – including what is happening around us, how we are feeling and what we are thinking. This takes practice. We are a society that is very caught up in the past, future or what is happening elsewhere. I bet when you look around at other children at school or on the bus it is hard to find one who is not glued to their phone. What mindfulness does is allow us to maintain stillness in an often chaotic or stressful world. Mindfulness is taking a step back from this chaos so that we can separate ourselves from it and get some space.

2. Introduce mindfulness meditation.

    Mindfulness meditation is a set of techniques designed to help us to become aware of what happens in our mind when we are not paying attention. There are so many things we do automatically (such as getting into a car or walking to school) that we often lose touch with the process of doing these things. We can go through much of the day in autopilot. Being mindful is making the decision to pay attention to these things in a certain way. Many people who think of meditation assume that people who meditate are trying to think of nothing. This is not true and isn't possible. Remember when we talked about how trying to avoid or push away certain thoughts can actually make them come back stronger. Mindfulness involves being aware of these thoughts, accepting them, and allowing them to flow freely. Instead of latching on to them, we give them space. You can practise mindfulness meditation anywhere and at any time of the day.

3. Facilitate a five-minute mindfulness meditation session.

Let's give it a shot. Get comfortable in your chair. Allow your body to start to relax. Close your eyes. Now I want you to pay attention to the way you are breathing. Start to slow down your breathing. Breathe in through the nose and then exhale through the nose or mouth. Allow your breath to go down into your diaphragm so that your stomach rises and falls. Relax and let the tension leave your body. It is normal to feel a little anxious or stressed when you start this. Just let yourself get into a rhythm. Keep breathing in through your nose and exhale slowly. You want to sit up in the chair and this will help the flow of air. Keep your shoulders relaxed.

[Guide the child to pay closer attention to the process.] *While you are breathing, notice the way your body feels – how the air feels coming into your body and how your body expands when the air comes in. If you notice your mind wandering off, gently bring your attention back to the present. Notice the body sensations, sounds and smells that may come up moment to moment. Don't try to find sounds or look for sensations, just be aware of anything that arises each moment without thinking too much about it.* [After a few minutes.] *Now pay attention to some of the thoughts that are coming up in your mind. Just look at them. Don't get stuck on them. Let them pass in and out of your mind freely. You are doing great. Now slowly open your eyes. How did you feel doing this?* [The child may report feeling a little anxious and frustrated. Explain that this is normal in the beginning, but that with practice, it becomes much easier.]

4. Discuss the value of practising mindfulness.

You will get better at being mindful the more you practise. If this is something that you would like to become good at, I suggest practising a little bit each day. Eventually you will have practised to the point where your body does this naturally. I would start to practise in small amounts of time. Five or ten minutes a day may be enough for you. In time you will be able to sit for longer periods of time. Try to avoid looking at the time while you are practising mindfulness meditation. This can be distracting. As you complete mindfulness meditation practice, allow yourself a few minutes to ease back into the everyday world. You might do this by sitting quietly for a few more minutes before you get up. You could also use this time to write in a journal or check in with yourself on how the practice was for you today.

Creative applications

- *Sticky notes on the brain.* Acquire a model brain or use something to represent the brain (e.g., a ball, hat, drawing, etc.). You can use the worksheet 'Sticky Notes on the Brain'. Using a pad of sticky notes, instruct the child to come up with as many unhelpful thoughts as she sometimes has. Write each of these on a sticky note and place it on the brain. Fill up the brain with sticky notes. Use this image to explain how the accumulation of negative or unhelpful thoughts and problems can become overwhelming and confusing. To relieve it of this build-up, take each sticky note and sort them into categories: (a) negative thoughts that can be discarded because they are untrue, (b) problems that are outside of one's control and so should not occupy the brain, (c) problems that need to be addressed later due to lack of sufficient resources (e.g., certain knowledge, energy) or because it is not an appropriate time to address them (e.g., trying to solve a relationship problem during a maths class), and (d) problems that can be solved now. You can incorporate the notion of *mindfulness* by saying that it is akin to being aware of these thoughts without being obligated to them. *Cognitive control* is the ability to sort and manage these thoughts, as well as to decide which to keep and which to discard.

CHAPTER 10
Making Healthy Lifestyle Choices

The topic of lifestyle choices, including diet, exercise and sleep, too often gets left out of child and adolescent therapy despite having important crosstalk with mental health. Proper self-care is one of the first things to go for many people who are affected by trauma. This can have a serious impact on mood and functioning. For example, poor sleep quality is associated with elevated symptoms of post-traumatic stress and is a risk factor for the development of child and adolescent anxiety problems (Babson, Badour, Feldner and Bunaciu 2012). Poor lifestyle habits can impose long-term health risks, as well as short-term functional impairment. Think about the last time you had little sleep, food and relaxation and felt stressed and overwhelmed. Did you have the energy and resources to deal with problems that came your way? Did you provide optimal therapy sessions? Now imagine if you made a habit of having little sleep, food and relaxation. The problems would get worse and harder to handle over time.

Children and adolescents are new to this game. They are actively learning about their bodies and how they should conduct themselves. It is important for them to receive the guidance necessary to make healthy lifestyle choices, which includes incorporating regular healthy behaviours into their day-to-day lives, as well as abstaining from or minimising behaviours that threaten health – such as alcohol and substance misuse. Emphasising to children the significance of these lifestyle choices on physical and psychological health and introducing a method of disciplining themselves to develop healthy lifestyle habits may go a long way. To this end, the following exercise offers suggestions for incorporating these objectives into therapy.

A HEALTHY LIFESTYLE

Goals

- To emphasise the importance of healthy lifestyle habits.
- To provide education and guidance about healthy lifestyle habits.
- To help the child to develop healthy lifestyle habits.

Procedure

1. Become familiar with the exercise and decide on the visual teaching tools you will use during the session.

2. *What to eat and when.* Explain how healthy eating can help to relieve stress and promote relaxation.

   The next thing I want to talk about is the benefit of healthy eating. What we eat can affect the way our body feels and our mood. The proper vitamins and minerals and high-fibre foods such as fruits, vegetables and wholegrains are critical and enable the body to respond to stress in a healthy way. What we might consider junk food or food that we should limit can have a negative effect on how the body responds to stress. These include having too much coffee, fizzy or other caffeinated drinks, sugary foods and drinks, and too many carbohydrates. Junk food may make us feel good in the very short term, but it is also related to higher stress levels, anxiety and negative mood. For example, sugar provides a quick boost of energy, but blood sugar falls drastically after the energy boost and can cause us to feel more tired and irritable than we were before we ate the sugary food. [Explore what kinds of foods the child eats.] *What kinds of foods do you find yourself eating? How do they affect the way you feel?* [Discuss the importance of eating on a regular schedule.] *It is also important to eat regular meals. Eating regular meals helps to stabilise our body and mood. It helps our body to be able to predict when it will be re-fuelled. Skipping meals or eating irregularly stresses the body and makes it less stable.*

3. *Keeping fit.* Explain the benefits of incorporating regular physical activity into the child's day-to-day activities. If you determine that the child is not getting enough daily physical activity, brainstorm ways of incorporating more activity into the child's day-to-day lifestyle and make a list of all of the ways the child can become physically active (see Figure 10.1).

   Being active and paying attention to your physical health is important in providing you with the resources to deal with stress, including dealing with memories of your past trauma. Physical activity gives us more energy, helps to relax us, helps us sleep better and lowers stress levels. Regular physical activity actually changes the biology and chemistry of our internal bodies to do these things. You don't have to be a pro athlete to benefit from regular physical activity. Simply finding time to walk on a daily basis can have huge health benefits. [Assess how much physical activity the child currently participates in on a daily basis.] *What kinds of physical activities do you get involved in?*

[Discuss whether this seems adequate or whether the child can increase his physical activity.]

4. *Getting sleep.* Discuss the importance of getting enough sleep and not sleeping too much on mood and coping.

Sleep is essential for our body and brain to function optimally. Too little sleep or too much sleep can cause us not to feel 100 per cent. What time do you usually go to bed? [Wait for response.] *And what time do you wake up in the morning?* [Wait for response.] *So you get about [x] hours of sleep at night. Are you happy with that amount? Does that work for you?* [If not, discuss what barriers might be interfering with sleep and how the child might overcome these barriers.] [If the child is having difficulty getting to sleep or staying asleep, discuss potential precipitators.] *Let's think about what you might do before going to sleep that will help you to fall asleep and to stay asleep. You can start thinking about these things a few hours before you go to bed. One of the things that can make it hard to fall asleep is caffeine. So, staying away from coffee, fizzy or soft drinks is critical.* [For adolescents.] *Other things that can make it hard to sleep include cigarettes and anything with nicotine. Drinking alcohol can also make for a bad night of sleep. Even though you may feel sleepy after drinking, it actually interrupts your sleep patterns and makes for a restless night. Eating a heavy meal a few hours before you go to sleep or eating any food immediately before going to sleep will also interfere with sleep patterns. Finally, a big one is watching TV, being on the computer, playing videogames or using your smartphone can surely make it hard to fall asleep – so you might try to stay away from these things at least an hour before you go to bed.* [Pause.] *There are things you can do to help your sleep quality.* [Discuss these, for example, exercise, reading, dimming the lights, relaxation techniques.]

Ways to Keep Active

- Walking around the block
- Dog walking
- Play a sport
- Jump rope
- Go swimming
- Plant and tend to a garden
- Ride a bike
- Take a hike in the woods
- Rollerblading or skateboarding
- Martial arts
- Play tug-of-war
- Climb a tree
- Jogging or running
- Push-ups and sit-ups
- Canoeing or kayaking
- Fly a kite
- Mow or rake a lawn
- Shovel snow
- Build something

FIGURE 10.1 WAYS TO KEEP ACTIVE

CHAPTER 11
Emotional Vocabulary and Awareness

Before language develops, the way children regulate their emotions involves crying, sucking and averting their gaze. Crying is an attempt to modify the child's situation by recruiting help. Sucking is a means of response modulation. Shifting gaze helps to re-allocate attention away from a negative stimulus. As language develops, so does the child's ability to identify and label emotions and to use their vocabulary to express how they feel and to seek comfort and support from caregivers and others. This ability paves the way for new emotion regulation strategies that necessitate a greater awareness of emotions and an emotional vocabulary. For example, a child who recognises that she is feeling extremely sad may influence an existing situation by choosing to eat lunch with her friends rather than eat alone where she is liable to dwell on a recent loss. In addition, children may actively modify their emotion reactions to an affectively charged stimulus. For example, a child who recognises that she is feeling afraid may reappraise the situation in a way that changes the emotional significance of the context by implementing cognitive change (e.g., 'I've done this many times and there's no reason to be afraid') or modifying her behavioural reactions (e.g., laughing out loud). As children develop they become more adept at selecting and utilising cognitive and behavioural strategies to regulate their emotions.

Children in less nurturing environments may have a deficient emotional vocabulary and may develop less adaptive ways of regulating their emotion. For example, children in families where there is an abundance of stressors including aggressive or chaotic patterns of interaction have a heightened level of distress, which may also contribute to the development of emotion suppression, deficits in emotion understanding and less adaptive coping strategies. In these types of environments, caregivers may be too unavailable or ill equipped to provide their children with support and modelling of healthy coping – instead modelling reactive or unhelpful emotional responses.

The purpose of this chapter is to provide guidance on assessing a child's emotional awareness and vocabulary and ways of increasing awareness and enriching the child's emotional vocabulary. These skills are essential for fully engaging in the therapeutic exposure and for processing the emotional content of the trauma memory.

THE FUNCTION OF EMOTION

Goals

- To emphasise the functional importance of emotion.
- To increase the child's awareness of her emotions.

Procedure

1. Decide on appropriate visual aids for explaining emotion.

2. Explain why emotion is important – even unpleasant emotions.

    Everyone has pleasant and unpleasant emotions. Sometimes we have them at the same time. Can you name some pleasant emotions? [Wait for response.] Good. Pleasant emotions tell us that we are doing well or that we are doing something right. Unpleasant emotions, such as sadness, anger, shame and fear, are unpleasant, but are also important. They tell us that something is wrong or needs our attention. Can you think of why that might be? [Wait for response.] For example, we might feel sad when we lose something or someone we care a lot about. When we express that we are sad it tells other people that we could use some support. If I saw someone crying I would feel the need to see what was the matter and possibly to help that person. Fear can tell us that there is possible danger. And even though anger can sometimes lead us to trouble, it can also help us to take action and to stand up for ourselves or other people when they are being wronged. Can you think of a time in the recent past when an unpleasant feeling was actually helpful to you because it made you aware of something that needed your attention? Take a minute to think about it. [Wait for response and discuss.]

3. Explain why avoiding unpleasant emotions is like ignoring important messages.

    A lot of times people try hard to ignore or push away unpleasant emotions. That is understandable, but we can miss what they are trying to tell us if we do this. Unpleasant emotions can upset us, overwhelm us, and we can get stuck in them. It takes a lot of energy to try to ignore these emotions. It is actually better to pay attention to them than to try to ignore them. If we pay attention to the unpleasant emotion and try to figure out what it is trying to tell us, we can start to address the real problem. It can be painful to go into a negative emotion and to listen and learn from it, but it is important to remember that it is temporary.

4. Describe the *cleaning the wound* analogy. This is a common one used to explain the rationale of therapeutic exposure and is well understood by children and adolescents.

    I want to give you an analogy. Pretend that an unpleasant emotion, such as sadness, is a cut on your skin or a wound. Let's say you fell off your bike and that your arm got cut up and that there is dirt and stuff in the cut. What would you want to do with the cut? [Let child respond.] Right, you would want to wash out the dirt so that it doesn't get infected. But that would hurt, wouldn't it? It would be much less painful if we put a bandage on it rather than clean it out. What would happen though if we did that? [Wait for response.] Right, it would become infected and it would hurt a lot more in the long run. The same thing can be said about unpleasant emotions. If we ignore them rather than deal with them head on, they can get infected and cause more problems later on. That is why it is important to pay attention to them and to 'clean them out'. Does that make sense? [Wait for response.]

5. Draw a connection to the unpleasant emotions felt when thinking about the trauma memory.

    Unpleasant emotions can come up when we think about a trauma memory. If we pay attention to these emotions then we can learn about why we have them and start to heal the pain caused by the trauma. If we ignore them, however, they fester and can get worse.

6. Explain the role of positive emotions.

    Sometimes people who have experienced a traumatic event have a harder time enjoying positive emotions. Negative emotions may be too strong and they might not be giving the positive emotions a chance to thrive. Sometimes we have to 'jump-start' the positive emotions so that they get stronger and get up and running again. Positive emotions can also quiet down the negative emotions or give us a break from them. What are some things you can do to increase positive emotions? [Let the child respond.] That's right. One important thing we can do is to surround ourselves with positive people. Sometimes when we are having a hard time, being around friends that make us laugh can give us a well-needed break from the problem. We can also make sure that we do things that we enjoy – even if the negative emotions are making us less interested in those things. Sometimes just starting to do them will remind us how much we enjoy them and the positive emotion will take over.

Creative applications

*   Collect a series of short video clips that elicit certain emotions. Play each of them with instructions for the child to pay attention to how she feels and to try to identify the emotion or emotions. Then work with the child to try to determine what these emotions are *telling* the child about what is happening in the video clip. Video clips are easily obtained online (e.g., YouTube, Vimeo).

*   Collect cartoon clippings from a newspaper or magazine that present a character feeling an unpleasant emotion. Talk about what the emotion is *telling* the character. Perhaps have the child draw her own cartoon or a series of cartoons related to this.

BUILDING AN EMOTIONAL VOCABULARY

Goals

- To assess the child's current emotional vocabulary.
- To enrich the child's emotional vocabulary.

Procedure

1. Using words from Table 11.1 and/or others you generate, compile a list of emotion words and put them in a format suitable for the child.

TABLE 11.1 EMOTION WORDS

Happy	Love	Defeated	Anxious	Outraged
Surprised	Helpless	Tenderness	Worried	Rage
Joyful	Powerless	Sympathy	Bored	Hostile
Cheerful	Dreading	Adoration	Rejected	Bitter
Content	Distrusting	Fondness	Disillusioned	Hateful
Proud	Suspicious	Receptive	Inferior	Scornful
Satisfied	Cautious	Interested	Grief-stricken	Spiteful
Excited	Disturbed	Shocked	Helpless	Vengeful
Amused	Overwhelmed	Exhilarated	Isolated	Disliked
Elated	Uncomfortable	Dismayed	Numb	Resentful
Optimistic	Guilty	Amazed	Regretful	Trusting
Enthusiastic	Hurt	Confused	Ambivalent	Distrusting
Delighted	Lonely	Stunned	Exhausted	Alienated
Calm	Melancholy	Interested	Fatigued	Insulted
Relaxed	Depressed	Intrigued	Insecure	Indifferent
Relieved	Hopeless	Absorbed	Disgusted	Captivated
Hopeful	Sad	Selfish	Pity	Shocked
Pleased	Guilty	Curious	Revulsion	Uncomfortable
Confident	Hurt	Anticipation	Contempt	Mindful
Brave	Lonely	Eager	Loathing	Peaceful
Comfortable	Regretful	Hesitant	Angry	Horrified
Safe	Sorrowful	Fearful	Jealous	Attentive

2. Explain why having an emotional vocabulary helps people to identify their emotions and to communicate to others how they feel.

    Why do you think we have words for emotions? [Wait for child to respond.] *That's right, being able to label how we feel and how other people feel helps us to communicate with each other. It's the same reason we have words for other things – such as colours. Even though you and I may not see the colour red in quite the same way, I can say, 'Hey, look at that red car over there', and you will know what I am talking about. In the same way, you and I may not feel 'angry', 'happy', or 'sad' in the same way, but you know what I mean if I say, 'I'm feeling a little sad today.'*

3. Assess the child's current emotion vocabulary by engaging the child in generating as many emotion words as she can think of. Let the child generate more of the words and fill in from your list as you see fit.

    Let's try something. Let's try to come up with as many words for feelings that we can come up with. We can make a list of them. Ready? Go. [Make a list on a piece of paper, poster board or on index cards.]

4. Make a distinction between emotion words and thoughts. Often children get the two confused.

    Is that an emotion word or is that a thought? Emotions can lead to thoughts and thoughts can lead to emotions, but they are a bit different. Emotions come from that emotion centre in our brains and thoughts come from the thinking centre.

Creative applications

*   Put the words on the backs of sticky notes and stick them to the wall or on a desk so that the word is concealed. After generating several emotion words, take turns choosing a sticky note and thinking about a specific time when you felt that emotion.

*   Make a personalised emotion chart. Either have the child draw pictures of facial expressions with corresponding emotion labels or get the caregiver's permission for the child to use the camera feature on a computer to take several pictures of her making different facial expressions. Arrange the pictures and label them with emotion words. Encourage the child to keep the chart and to share it with her caregiver. This can also be something that the child and caregiver do as a conjoint activity.

*   Make an emotion colour or texture wheel. Have the child match colour or texture (e.g., lines, patterns) to each emotion word. A number of well-known visual artists have used colour and texture to represent emotion and other abstractions such as music (e.g., Roy De Maistre, Wassily Kandinsky). These artists' works are easily found online and you might explore these with the child. See Figure 11.1 as an example of the use of texture to represent emotion.

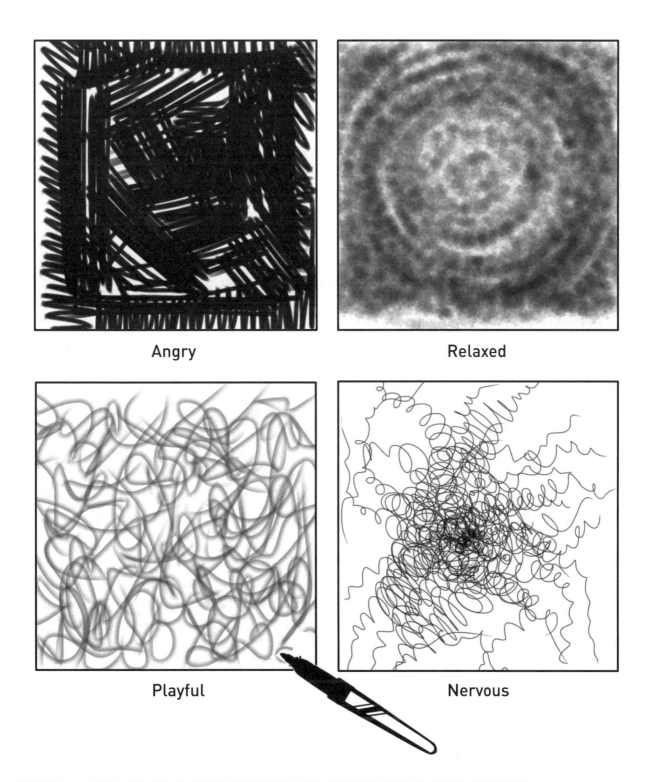

Angry

Relaxed

Playful

Nervous

FIGURE 11.1 EXAMPLES OF USING TEXTURE TO REPRESENT EMOTION WORDS

CHAPTER 12
Tolerating Trauma Work

This component involves reviewing and applying all of the knowledge and skills introduced to the child in order to prepare him to focus on the trauma specifically. This is a scary part of the therapy for many children. It means they will have to think about and potentially talk about the traumatic event – something they have been working so hard to avoid and get away from. However, you will have been providing subtle forms of therapeutic exposure up to this point and so some habituation may have taken place.

It is vital to revisit the rationale for doing the trauma work and to rekindle the child's motivation for following through with it. This is a fragile time in the therapy process. Dropout rates are highest prior to therapeutic exposure and/or trauma memory processing. The child will require a lot of support from you, as well as from his caregiver. This is also a time that threatens the therapeutic alliance between you and the child. The child may feel threatened and try to sabotage the relationship in order to avoid engaging in exposure or trauma memory processing. It is important that you properly align the level of avoidance and resistance the child is presenting and the level of therapeutic exposure and/or trauma memory processing you plan to facilitate. However, the latter should not be so diluted that it renders the technique ineffective. The optimal goal is to work with the child to be able to tolerate the full intensity of the therapeutic exposure and trauma memory processing. This may necessitate a stepwise approach.

BUILDING A TOLERANCE

Goals

- To revisit the rationale for therapeutic exposure and/or trauma memory processing.
- To encourage the child to use the knowledge and skills obtained thus far to tolerate the trauma work.
- To point out that the strong therapeutic alliance you and the child have developed will help ease the distress associated with the trauma work.
- To frame tolerance as an achievable challenge for children deserving of praise and commendation.

Procedure

1. Become familiar with the module and decide on the visual teaching tools you will use during the session.

2. Review with the child the rationale behind therapeutic exposure. Refer to Chapter 6. Answer any questions the child may have.

3. Encourage the child to use all of the resources he has realised and established to tolerate the distress and discomfort that comes with therapeutic exposure and trauma memory processing.

   Earlier we talked about all of the strengths and resources that you are fortunate to have. Also, for the past several weeks [or months] you have worked very hard to learn a lot of material and gain a number of skills. These are useful in everyday life for anyone; however, these will be particularly helpful to you for working with me on this next component of therapy. It is very normal to be anxious and stressed about starting this phase of therapy. I want to reassure you, though, that I am confident you have what it takes to move forward with this. Which of the skills and strategies that you learned do you think will help the most? [Wait for response.]

4. Point out that you and the child have developed a strong working relationship and that this will help ease the distress associated with the trauma work.

   Remember when we talked about the importance of social resources when dealing with stress? I want to point out that since we started to meet together we have developed a rather strong working relationship. Would you agree? [Wait for response.] I feel like I have got to know you and I hope that you feel you can trust me and use me as a resource. I will help you through this next step in therapy. One way I plan to do that is by carefully choosing how we will go about doing the therapeutic exposure work. Your input will also be important as we move forward.

   That said, I also want to point out that it is quite normal to become frustrated or upset when doing the trauma work. You might even feel angry or upset at me for encouraging you to do it. That is all totally fine and normal. You have my permission to get angry or upset at me at any point in time. However, I encourage you to talk to me about it when it happens because it is part of the important work. You also might have some strong feelings that you didn't realise you would have. This is normal too. Again, let's talk about these when they happen. I will do my best to recognise when you are having these feelings and will help you through them. Do you have any questions or concerns about what we just talked about?

5. Motivate and challenge the child to feel empowered to engage in the trauma work.

    I wouldn't encourage you to do this work if I didn't think you were ready for it. You are ready. You have what it takes to do very well with this. I'm not saying that it is going to be a piece of cake – it will be challenging at times; but you will meet this challenge. I have confidence. How confident in yourself do you feel right now?

6. Describe the challenge as praiseworthy.

    When you are finished with this phase of therapy, you will no doubt feel very proud of yourself – as will I and your parent(s) [or whomever is the child's family support]. [Sometimes therapists and/or caregivers do something special upon completion of the therapy to commemorate the achievement – such as having pizza or cake at the session or some other reward.] *When we are finished, we will celebrate your achievement by...* [whatever is decided].

PART 3

Trauma Work with the Child

CHAPTER 13
Starting the Trauma Work

At this point in therapy you should have a good sense of the child's level of avoidance of the trauma and her resistance to the upcoming trauma work. Your job now is to determine the best methods for facilitating therapeutic exposure and/or trauma memory processing. One option is to start big and scale down. That is, attempt to engage the child in more intensive therapeutic exposure and scale down as necessary. Another option is to use the information that you have gathered thus far to decide the best level of therapeutic exposure. There is no existing scale that characterises exposure techniques as mild, moderate or intense. In fact, it would be difficult to do this given that individuals will respond differently to the same experience. However, the following chapters attempt to provide some guidance on ways you might increase or decrease the intensity of certain techniques. There is also no way reliably to measure a child's level of avoidance and resistance to exposure. You will have to use your best judgement. There are, however, some tips that you can use to help make this judgement. The first exercise in this part of the resource provides guidance on how to gather information about the child's level of avoidance/resistance in order to choose the best starting point for this phase of treatment. The next discusses some preparatory steps you might take prior to the actual exposure session.

It will take the child time to build up sufficient trust with you to share the personal nature of the trauma experience. It is not only fear of thinking about the traumatic experience that contributes to a child's avoidance, but also the fear of having to talk about personal matters with you, especially having to do with sexuality in the case of sexual abuse or assault. For example, consider the male adolescent with a significant history of childhood sexual abuse who thwarted attempts to engage in Imaginal Exposure because he felt intense shame and embarrassment narrating the details of the times the perpetrator raped and sodomised him. You should acknowledge this common barrier and openly discuss the child's worries about having to talk about this material with you. Remember how awkward or uncomfortable you might have felt when having to have the *sex talk* with one of your parents – or if you are a parent, how it might have been for your child. Now imagine how much harder it would be to have to share the details of a sexual act with an adult, and especially one in which you were a victim of abuse. You can help ease the child's anxieties by maintaining good rapport with the child, but also by acknowledging the child's anxiety, emphasising that it is a common worry, and developing a vocabulary for how to talk about the details of the trauma. For example, in the case of sexual trauma, showing the child that you can say sexual words (e.g., penis, vagina, masturbate) will model for the child that it is okay to use them. Also, acknowledging that you understand the child's hesitation and reassuring the child that you have had these conversations with other children and adolescents and that you are not judging her in any way will make it more comfortable for children to communicate with you.

MEASURING DISTRESS

Goal

- To establish a metric for measuring the child's distress that will be used during therapeutic exposure and in-vivo exposure.

Procedure

1. Establishing a metric for measuring the child's distress is a common practice of many therapies for anxiety, as well as PTSD. There are several graphical templates for measuring distress, including the classic fear thermometer. The fear thermometer is good because it offers a useful metaphor for children who have had some experience with measuring temperature. However, you may find that there is a better metaphor for the particular child you are working with. Use your creativity when designing the distress metric, as you will likely use it throughout the therapy. You might find that having the child design and create the graphical template helps to engage the child and ensure that she understands the way in which distress is being measured. When creating the template it is important to establish the measurement's anchors. What does '0' mean? What does '10' or '100' mean? The worksheet 'Distress Scale' provides a standard fear thermometer template and Figure 13.1 provides a number of examples of self-designed templates.

2. Explain the concept of measuring distress and how it will be used in therapy.

   Today I want to work with you on figuring out a way of measuring your distress or how upset you feel at any moment in time. The reason we want to do this is so that we can track your level of distress at different times during the programme. Have you ever put a number on how upset you felt before? [Wait for response.] It is a useful way of looking at changes in distress levels.

3. Provide the option of having the child create her own template.

   What I want to do is to come up with a distress scale that can be put on paper so that we can use it several times over the course of the programme. We can use one that is already made or you can create your own. As you are pretty talented at art, I figured you might want to make your own.

4. Establish the anchors of the measure.

   The first thing you need to decide is the range of the scale. In other words, will it go from 0–10 or 0–100? I suggest that you don't go any less than 10 and no more than 100. [Wait for child to respond.] Okay, good. The next thing is to decide how you want to design the scale. A lot of people use a picture of a thermometer because it is convenient to think of being distressed as being hot and being calm as being cool. However, you can use whatever you want. Another idea is to draw a cup filled with different levels of water or 'distress'. Think about it for a minute and decide what you want to go with.

5. Make several copies of the template.

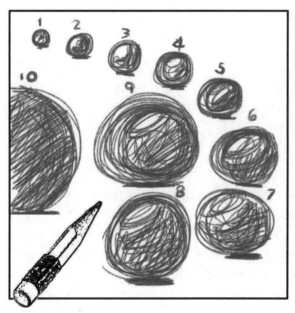

Example 1

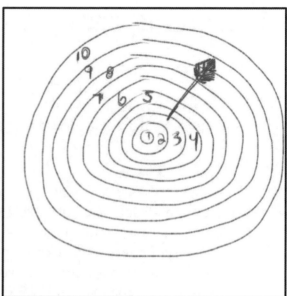

Example 2

Example 3

FIGURE 13.1 EXAMPLES OF CHILD-CREATED DISTRESS SCALES

ESTABLISHING A BASELINE

Goals

- To assess the child's level of avoidance and resistance to therapeutic exposure.
- To assess the child's ability to provide detail, including specific feelings and thoughts.
- To prompt a discussion with the child regarding her concerns about therapeutic exposure.

Procedure

1. Determine how you plan to conduct the baseline exposure. If you are using TF-CBT, the general protocol is to have the child narrate the event while you type or write it out. The child could also choose to write it out on her own and then read it aloud. In TF-CBT this can happen early in therapy or immediately prior to the trauma narrative development. In Prolonged Exposure the equivalent to this happens during the assessment and information-gathering sessions.

2. Introduce the child to the exercise. You might explain that it is a preview of what therapeutic exposure will entail and a chance to discuss any concerns or questions the child has, or that it is a chance for you to better understand what happened to the child, and what she was feeling and thinking at the time.

   As I mentioned last week, we are going to do what is often called the 'baseline narrative' today. First, we will do a relaxation exercise so that you feel comfortable and relieved from the day's stress. Then I will ask you to go through the traumatic event [or the child's perceived worst traumatic event if there were multiple] from beginning to end in as much detail as possible. I would like you to do this in first person, present tense. This means that you would say something like, 'I hear the alarm clock going off next to the bed and I wake up. My eyes are still closed. I don't want to open them.' While you are doing this I will type what you say. Try to include things you might have been feeling at the time or things you might have been thinking. Go slow and try to be as detailed as possible.

3. Get a rating of the child's distress level at the beginning and at three- to five-minute intervals. In Prolonged Exposure you are using the 0–100 subjective units of distress scale (SUDS). Every few minutes you might ask for another rating. This will allow you to plot the child's distress over that period. This is useful in that it provides you with the child's subjective pattern of distress, and provides the child with a visual representation of her emotional response.

4. Facilitate the relaxation exercise.

   Okay, let's begin the relaxation exercise. [Three- to five-minutes.]

5. Present the child the option of leaving her eyes open or closing them. Have the child begin.

Okay. Now you can close your eyes or leave them open – your choice. I am not going to interrupt you except to ask you to rate your stress level like I did a few minutes ago. Do you have any questions before you start? Okay, go ahead.

6.   Ask the child how she felt doing this exercise.

Great job. Now, open your eyes. Take a deep breath. Now I want to ask you how it was for you to do this exercise. How did it feel? [Allow child to respond.] Is there anything you felt or thought that you were surprised about or didn't expect? [Wait for response.]

7.   If the child generally tolerated the exercise, praise her for being able to do this initial exercise. If the child did not tolerate the exercise well, either discontinuing or becoming too emotionally distressed to continue, then conduct a relaxation exercise and normalise the experience.

[If child tolerated] Even though it was uncomfortable to do this, you actually did a fine job. I am impressed. [If child did not tolerate the exercise well.] That was difficult for you. It is completely normal to have very strong feelings during this exercise. You avoided thinking and talking about this experience for so long. When you finally allow yourself to take a look at it, strong feelings come out. Let's do a relaxation exercise. [Conduct relaxation exercise.]

8.   Go over the child's distress ratings. Point out where the ratings peak and highlight this as a particularly distressing part of the narrative. If the ratings are generally low, talk about why the exercise may not have elicited strong feelings. It may be that the child can communicate what happened without emotionally connecting with it. These children are very good 'avoiders'.

Let's take a look at your distress ratings. The nice thing about these is that it allows us to measure your emotional responses to the trauma. These will be an important way to monitor how the therapy is coming along. [Discuss.]

9.   Address any of the child's concerns and answer any questions.

I want to ask you if doing this exercise raised any worries or concerns you might have or brought up any questions that I can answer. [Wait for response and discuss.]

TALKING ABOUT SEXUAL MATERIAL

Goals

- To validate and ease the child's discomfort sharing personal information.
- To establish a vocabulary for talking about sexual material.
- To build the child's trust in you as a recipient of personal information.

Procedure

1. Acknowledge that many children feel uncomfortable talking about sexual material.

    I realise that it can be very hard for a child to talk to an adult about sex and sexual material, especially when it has to do with sexual assault. I want to let you know that I have worked with many children who have been sexually assaulted and all of them have had difficulty with this. As the therapeutic exposure I talked to you about involves sharing details of the sexual trauma, I want to talk about how we can make it more comfortable for you to share this information. The first thing I want to point out is that I have talked to several girls and boys about sexual trauma and nothing we talk about will be something I haven't heard already from someone else. I will not judge you or think badly of you in any way. Is this something that you have been thinking or worrying about? [Wait for child's response.]

2. Encourage the child to feel comfortable asking you questions.

    Also, I do not expect you to know everything there is to know about sexuality or sexual body parts. I see children who have had different amounts of education about sex. Some have had no sex education. Others have had a lot. What I am saying is that it is okay if you do not know something and I encourage you to feel comfortable asking me about it.

3. Establish a vocabulary for talking about trauma-relevant sexual body parts and sexual behaviour.

    It is also important for us to be comfortable using the scientific names for body parts and sexual behaviour. Our body, including our sexual body, is something that we should respect. There is no shame in it. I am in favour of calling it what it is. If it's the male sex organ, it makes sense to call it the penis. If it's the female sex organ, it's appropriate to call it the vagina. If we're referring to having sex, it can be called intercourse or sexual penetration. If it's self-stimulation, we can use the words masturbation. I want to let you know that I am comfortable using these words and my hope is that you feel just as comfortable using them when we start to process the trauma memory. I am also familiar with other ways of saying these things – and if that is how you know it, use whatever words you know. I may suggest another way of saying it. The important thing is for you to know that it is okay to say it. If you're unsure about something, or don't know how to say something, that's totally fine. Let's figure it out together, okay?

CHAPTER 14
Indirect Therapeutic Exposure

Exposure is not easy. In fact, it can be terrifying. No matter how hard you try, some children will not comply with it. This might mean modifying the protocol to do as much therapeutic exposure and processing as possible without reaching the tipping point at which the child refuses to return to therapy. It is not always easy to know exactly what that threshold is. The best approach to take with a highly avoidant child is to take a gradual but steady approach into the exposure work. For some children, the anticipation of doing the exposure work causes more anxiety than the exposure itself. Take a stepwise approach. Each step should challenge the child, but also reassure the child that he can tolerate and benefit from the work. Each step should increase the child's self-confidence, as well as his confidence and trust in you. It will take the child time to build up sufficient trust to share the personal nature of the trauma experience.

The indirect techniques featured in this chapter are meant to facilitate therapeutic exposure and processing by *exposing* the child to aspects of his own trauma memory through the eyes of another child. In other words, the idea is to use another child's experience to encourage the child you are working with to think about his own traumatic experience in meaningful ways. Use caution with this exercise as you do not want to prompt or lead a child to adopt details of the example narrative as his own – in effect, developing a false memory. Thus, use broad examples and stress to the child that it is an example from another child's experience. Also, this technique should not be used when the trauma is suspected, but not confirmed. This may be a stepping-stone to more intensive trauma work, or it may be the only way the child will do any therapeutic exposure and trauma memory processing. After all, relaxing the standard approach to therapeutic exposure in order to do *some* trauma work with the child is better than not getting anything done at all because the child and family dropped out of therapy or the child shuts down and refuses to engage with you.

WORKING WITH A MOCK TRAUMA NARRATIVE

Goals

- Develop a narrative that resembles the traumatic experience of the child.
- Use the 'Mock Narrative' worksheet to function as a lead into the child's own trauma memory.
- Motivate the child to create his own trauma narrative.

Procedure

1. Develop a narrative that features the following:

   The same type of trauma as the child you are working with.

   The narrator is the same sex.

   A carefully crafted narration of the event in the first person, present tense.

   Examples of the use of emotion words to express how the child is feeling.

   Examples of thoughts and internal dialogue.

   A section that reflects how the child feels and thinks about the traumatic event *now*.

2. Several 'Mock Narratives' are provided as worksheets. These are inspired by actual trauma narratives but feature fictional cases.

   'Witnessing Physical Assault and Loss': Carla is an adolescent girl who witnessed her brother being physically assaulted by a group of other boys in her neighbourhood. Her brother suffered fatal injuries and was pronounced dead at the hospital. Carla opted to write her narrative in the form of a poem.

   'Domestic Violence': Rafael is an 11-year-old boy who witnessed severe domestic violence between his mother and his stepfather. The worst incident and the focus of his narrative was when his stepfather beat his mother to the ground, threw a bottle at her and kicked her. She required medical care. Rafael attempted to intervene by posturing at his stepfather. In response, his stepfather threw him against the wall. He then went for help from the neighbours in the next apartment.

   'Serious Car Accident': Bridgett is a 12-year-old girl who was in a serious car accident involving her grandmother and another vehicle. A child in the other vehicle died on the scene. Bridgett's grandmother suffered critical injuries but survived.

   'Child Sexual Abuse': Kyle is a 14-year-old boy with a history of sexual abuse by a male friend of the family who had babysat for him between the ages of seven and eight. Kyle only revealed the abuse about a year ago. Kyle also has experienced other adversity including family drug and alcohol problems and having unstable housing.

   'Group Sexual Assault': Jenna is a 16-year-old teenager who was raped by a group of older boys in a park near school. The assault happened less than a year ago.

'Natural Disaster': Jamie is a 12-year-old boy whose family lost their home due to a tornado. After the storm Jamie was the first to witness an elderly neighbour who had been dismembered and killed by the impact of a vehicle wrapped around a tree in the yard.

'School Shooting': Natalia is an eight-year-old girl who was a student at a school where a gunman unexpectedly walked in and killed several students and teachers before taking his own life. Natalia's class was spared but she heard the gunshots and the screams happening in the classroom next door.

3. Put the narrative into a format that will be well received by the child. For a younger child it may be a small booklet with illustrated pages. For an older child it may be done with a computer or made to look like a comic book. This is where your creativity comes in.

4. Introduce the 'Mock Narrative' to the child.

    I brought in something to share with you today. It is a trauma narrative that another [boy/girl] created. I chose it because of how similar [his/her] story is to yours. [If needed, explain that the child agreed to use his/her narrative to help other children develop theirs.]

5. Point out where the *mock* child uses emotion words to express feelings.

    I want to point out this sentence here where it says, 'I feel terrified because I think he is coming back.' See how [he/she] is using [his/her] emotion vocabulary to express how [he/she] was feeling at the time?

6. Point out where the *mock* child identifies his/her thoughts.

    See this where [he/she] says, 'I am thinking that I will never get out of this alive.' This is important because [he/she] has identified the thoughts that [he/she] had at the time of the trauma.

7. At any point in time, continue discussing the child's own trauma experience if the situation calls for it. Look for cues from the child that indicates a lead into the child's experience. Any 'I' statements from the child are good leads.

[Child]	*That's not how I felt when that happened to me.*
[Therapist]	*No? How did you feel?*
[Child]	*I was more...angry I guess.*
[Therapist]	*That's a good observation. Was there anything else you felt along with angry? [Use this as an opportunity to get the child to talk. Refrain from trying to explain or interpret the difference. Use prompts to elicit more from the child.]*

CHAPTER 15
Low-level Therapeutic Exposure

In this chapter, low-level therapeutic exposure includes developing a written trauma narrative, reading the trauma narrative aloud and listening to the trauma narrative being read by the therapist with or without the child's eyes closed. There is no hard and fast rule about what is low vs. high-level exposure. Part of that depends on the child. For some children, simply writing the trauma narrative will be quite intense. For others, writing the trauma narrative may not fully *activate* the trauma memory. What is true, however, is that children tend to choose the method that is least threatening – and as avoidance is the hallmark feature of PTSD, eschewing intense exposure work for an exercise that permits more *distance* from the trauma memory is common. Therefore, aim high knowing that the arrow will hit lower.

For the purpose of this book, high-level therapeutic exposure is considered fully engaging in Imaginal Exposure such that the child's eyes are closed and she is visualising and narrating the trauma memory in the first person, present tense. As mentioned earlier, there is no research to suggest that Imaginal Exposure is more effective, per se, than writing a trauma narrative. However, Imaginal Exposure is designed to engage the sensory system as fully as possible in the context of a visualisation exercise. This is consistent with the theory underlying therapeutic exposure more generally across the spectrum of anxiety disorders.

In Prolonged Exposure, the Imaginal Exposure is tempered when a patient is *over-engaged* or in such distress that the patient is hyperventilating, can no longer engage with the therapist or has lost control of her behaviour. Typically the exposure is tempered by modifying the protocol such that the therapist allows the patient to leave her eyes open or builds in breathing exercises or other strategies to help the patient remain calm and grounded. The therapist also more frequently reminds the patient that she is in the safety of a therapy office and that she is *not* re-experiencing the trauma.

When making the decision to conduct Imaginal Exposure or to engage the child in developing a written narrative, it is not as easy as using the patient's age as a determining factor. There is nothing to suggest that Imaginal Exposure is best for an adult whereas developing a written narrative is best for a child. Although it may be difficult for young children to engage in a visualisation exercise because of their developmental immaturity, there is no data to suggest that adult patients who receive Prolonged Exposure and do Imaginal

Exposure are better off than patients who receive CPT and develop written narratives. It is more nuanced than that. In fact, much is driven by a patient's preferences and the therapist's proficiency at conducting the therapy. To that end, you will have to choose the approach that seems the best fit for your patient.

STARTING THE TRAUMA NARRATIVE

Goals

- To begin therapeutic exposure.
- To use the child's creativity to motivate her engagement in creating the trauma narrative.

Procedure

1. Create a menu of options for the child to choose from regarding how she will create the trauma narrative product, as well as how the child might begin the planning process.

2. Introduce the child to her options for making the trauma narrative and use the child's talent (e.g., drawing, music) or interests (e.g., computers) to motivate her.

   There are so many ways that you can decide to make your trauma narrative. Everyone makes his or hers a little different. One child I worked with made his trauma narrative in the form of a comic book. Another one turned it into a rap song. Someone else made a computer presentation. I also saw someone narrate theirs as a short video clip. Take a minute and think about how you see doing your trauma narrative. [You can also use the 'Mock Narratives' as inspirational examples.]

3. Make a list of any materials you will need.

4. Brainstorm or outline the material. This might involve having the child think of a title for each of the chapters or how the narrative will be structured. All of this can and often changes, but it helps the child to start thinking about the content.

   Let's think of some of the titles of your chapters. What will you call the first chapter? [Let child respond.] Okay. Let me write this down – 'Life before the trauma'. Good, what do you think will come after this?

Creative applications

- Make a timeline that encompasses the time period of the traumatic experience. Have the child start by remembering significant events or changes. Sometimes making a timeline helps to organise the trauma memory and to demarcate a start and finish.

- Have the child use free association to generate words, thoughts or images related to the trauma. Then decide on a way to organise what the child generated into categories or in a temporal sequence.

- Have the child start to link her feelings with the trauma memory by generating emotion words, organising emotion cards, or using colour to reflect her emotions. For example, you might instruct the child to start by applying the background colour of what will represent the traumatic event, then use this as a starting point to prompt for other feelings and thoughts related to the situation.

- Start by having the child draw pictures that will accompany the narrative with plans to add in the written content later.

DEVELOPING THE NARRATIVE

Goals

- To sustain the child's motivation to continue working on the narrative.
- To proceed with therapeutic exposure.
- To overcome barriers.

Procedure

1. Show the child that you are committed to the narrative development and eager to continue. Commonly, children will resist returning to the narrative. Although they may have had a successful session the week before, several days have gone by and some anxiety and avoidance has crept back up. Be positive and persistent. Try to make the trauma narrative a challenge rather than a chore. Praise the child for her good work after each session. You also might consider talking to the caregiver about implementing other incentives (e.g., eating at a favourite restaurant after the session) if it helps to keep the child positive and cooperative.

2. Move at a steady pace. The child may resist moving on to more challenging parts of the narrative development. Be supportive but directive with the child. Remind the child that she has a goal to reach and that she is doing great so far. Having established a good working rapport with the child up to this point will help to minimise any pushback from the child.

3. Make it a goal for the child to fill out the trauma narrative so that you and the child can start the process of re-reading and revising the narrative. Remember, the product itself is not the ultimate goal. Rather, it is the iterative process of going over the trauma material with the child that will facilitate habituation and processing.

THE ITERATIVE PROCESS

Goals

- To conduct multiple therapeutic exposures.
- To facilitate cognitive and emotional processing of the trauma memory.

Procedure

1. Make it clear to the child that reviewing the trauma narrative again and again is not only necessary for revision, but also to facilitate the therapeutic exposure.

2. You might have the child keep track of how many times she has gone through the trauma narrative by making hash marks and recording her level of distress. This is particularly motivating for children with a competitive drive. Plus, you can track these numbers and hopefully be able to show the child a reduction in distress over time.

3. For one or more of the iterations, instruct the child to read it, this time inserting statements about how she felt at the time. Look for opportunities to suggest inserting an emotion statement.

   [Therapist]   *How did you feel after you found the body?*

   [Child]   *Sick to my stomach. Grossed out. Shocked, I guess.*

4. For one or more of the iterations, instruct the child to read through the narrative and insert statements about what she was thinking at the time. Again, look for opportunities to suggest inserting a thought statement.

   [Therapist]   *Can I ask a question? What was going through your mind at that moment when you saw him throw hot coffee at your mother?*

   [Child]   *I was thinking that I wished I was strong enough to kill him.*

5. Look for statements that might reflect an unhealthy thought or distortion (e.g., 'I am forever ruined by the rape. I should never have trusted him'). When you find one of these, use Socratic questioning and basic cognitive behavioural techniques to explore the thought further and to challenge the thought.

6. Look for opportunities to explore the child's relationship with someone who has a role in the trauma narrative. An important aspect of processing the trauma memory has to do with understanding how the trauma has affected the child's relationship with others in her life. You might prompt the child with questions that may explore this.

   Tell me about your relationship with your father. You haven't said much about how he felt about the sexual abuse. What was his reaction? [Allow child to respond.] How do you think the sexual abuse has affected your relationship with your dad?

7. Point out times in the narrative when the child did something worthy of praise or recognition (e.g., contacted emergency personnel, removed a sibling from the domestic violence, told about the abuse).

I want to pause for a second to point out how courageous you were when you stood up for your younger brother like that and brought him to the neighbour's house. It truly shows how devoted you are as a sister, and how reliable you are. I bet your brother thinks the world of you. What do you think about that?

8. Look for areas in which the child could provide additional detail. Instruct the child to focus on what kinds of things she felt, saw, heard or smelled in order to elaborate on the context in which the trauma occurred. It may help for the child to close her eyes.

[Therapist] *Okay. Wait a sec. Take a step back for a moment. I'm wondering if you can really explain to me what it was like to be there at that moment. Try to paint a picture for someone who was not there and has no idea what it was like. What kinds of sounds did you hear around you? What did you smell at the time? What did the ground feel like? It will help if you close your eyes. Really 'go there' in your mind and describe what it was like on the street that day the accident happened.*

[Child] *It was hard to see because the sun was glaring off the windows. I smelled peanuts. Yeah, there was a guy selling roasted peanuts on the corner. It also smelled, well, dirty I guess. The city can have a dirty smell to it. I remember seeing a newspaper blowing in the wind and I remember hitting it with my foot. I heard taxis blowing their horns as they always do. There were people talking on their phones. I think there was some guy yelling something about religion or something coming from behind. Then it all happened in a flash.*

SHARING THE NARRATIVE WITH A CAREGIVER

Goals

- To establish an open line of communication between the child and caregiver regarding the trauma.
- To expose the child to parental support and praise for doing the trauma work.

Procedure

1. Prior to facilitating the conjoint session you have already worked with the caregiver to prepare them to listen to the narrative and to provide the child with praise and reinforcement. You should already have determined that the caregiver is ready to listen to the child share the narrative and will respond in a therapeutic manner. In addition, the child has agreed to share the narrative with the caregiver and wants to do it. If the child does not want to share the narrative, there may be good reason.

2. Check in with the caregiver and child individually prior to bringing them together in a conjoint session. Are there any last minute concerns? It may help to have the parent listen to the narrative and have the child read the narrative immediately prior to the conjoint session.

3. Ensure that the child and caregiver are comfortable. You might have them do a relaxation exercise together prior to the narrative sharing.

4. In general, let the session take its course. Do not remove yourself completely, but take a back seat. Allow the child to take her time reading the narrative. Avoid interrupting unless the situation calls for therapist intervention. For example, consider one conjoint session in which the child had just arrived at the most emotionally intense part of her narrative about paternal sexual abuse when the mother's mobile phone dinged and she proceeded to return a text message. The therapist paused the child until she had the mother's full attention again. Most of the time, though, a caregiver will provide the child with positive feedback and praise. If a caregiver is struggling with this, you might provide some cues (e.g., 'Brynn worked very hard on this, and what a wonderful job she did, wouldn't you say?').

CHAPTER 16
High-level Therapeutic Exposure

For some adolescents developing the trauma narrative may not fully access the emotional components of the trauma memory, resulting in what is referred to in Prolonged Exposure as *under-engagement*. When a patient is under-engaged, he is able to narrate the trauma in adequate detail, but is emotionally disconnected or dissociated with the trauma memory. This may or may not be evident by the child's distress ratings, as some under-engaged patients report high distress ratings but present as having low distress by virtue of their tone of voice and body language. Remember that many of these children are very good at disconnecting from the trauma as a way of avoiding the distress that comes with it. When you suspect under-engagement, it is time to think about revisiting the exposure approach.

Imaginal Exposure may help to *activate* the emotional aspects of the trauma memory as it involves closing one's eyes and narrating the trauma memory in the first person, present tense. You can further foster emotional engagement by probing the child for additional details, sights, smells, sounds, tactile sensations, thoughts and feelings. It is important, however, for you to keep some distance from the visualisation so as not to interrupt the child's connection to the imagery. Thus, prompt using brief questions that are timed appropriately following a child's statement. Time the questions so that they do not invite the child to have a conversation with you. The goal is to keep him connected to the imagery, and to enhance it.

The exercise that follows is designed to help you to enhance the therapeutic exposure by following an Imaginal Exposure protocol and employing strategies to strengthen the child's emotional connection to the imagery.

IMAGINAL EXPOSURE

Goal

- To fully activate the emotional components of the trauma memory.

Procedure

1. Briefly review the rationale for Imaginal Exposure.

2. Review the procedure.

   Okay. The Imaginal Exposure will last about 30 to 45 minutes. When we begin I will ask you to close your eyes and to make yourself comfortable. I want you to know that I will not be staring at you. I will be looking down at my pad. I will ask you to begin and you will start at the beginning of your trauma memory. [Decide on where that will be prior to beginning the Imaginal Exposure.] You will use what we call first person narration. This means that you will be talking as you, and using words such as 'I am', 'My body' and 'Me'. You will also use what we call present tense. This means you will be talking as though the thing is happening right now; for example, 'I am feeling comfortable', 'My body is shaking', 'The rain is falling on me.' If you switch into past tense, which many people do without realising it, I will gently remind you to talk as though it is happening now. Try to think about all of the details of your experience. By this I mean, as you are visualising the experience, pay close attention to the way things look, smell, sound and feel. Pay attention to all of your senses. I might remind you of this at times. Also, pay attention to any emotions you might be having and any kinds of thoughts that come to mind. Include these in your narration. If you tell the trauma memory from start to finish and time is not quite up, I will ask you to start again. Keep your eyes closed and simply go back to the beginning of the trauma memory and start again. Finally, I will ask you every three to five minutes what your distress rating is. Remember, the distress rating is from 1 to 10 [or whatever you and the child agreed upon]. Don't open your eyes, but simply give me the rating and continue on. Okay? [Wait for response.]

3. Start the Imaginal Exposure.

4. Correct the child when he slips into past tense by saying something like, 'Remember to talk as though it is happening now.'

5. Occasionally prompt for more detail by drawing attention to sensory perceptions; for example, 'What do you hear? Is there a certain smell in the air? Are there sounds in the background? What can you see? What does it feel like?'

6. Occasionally prompt for emotion statements; for example, 'What are you feeling right now?' Do not suggest an emotion. For example, do not say, 'Are you feeling anxious now?' Let the child generate his own emotion words.

7. Occasionally prompt for thought statements; for example, 'What are you thinking about? What kinds of thoughts are going through your head? What are you saying to yourself?' Again, do not suggest thoughts. Let the child generate his own thought statements.

8. Collect distress ratings. Make the questions short, simple and unobtrusive. Try to insert them in between the child's statements and in places least likely to interrupt the flow of the exposure. 'From 1 to 10, what is your rating now?' You may need to remind and encourage the child to keep his eyes closed.

9. If the child begins to cry, allow him to do so. You might tell him that it is perfectly fine to cry while doing the exposure. If the crying seems to be keeping the child from continuing, you might say something to the effect of, 'I see that you are crying and that is just fine. Don't let that stop you from continuing. Crying can be a good thing. It shows that the exposure is doing what it is supposed to do.'

10. If the child becomes excessively emotionally distressed, then it may be necessary to take him down a notch. One clue that a child may be excessively distressed is if you think that the child has gone beyond the point of being capable of learning. Another indication is if it looks as if the child is experiencing the trauma memory as though it were actually happening – with little to no awareness of the context of the therapy office. For example, a child may not respond to your prompt or your request for a distress rating. This can happen with children who are particularly dissociative. This phenomenon is more common in children with a history of sexual abuse. Dissociative children have a hard time maintaining self-control and staying grounded in the present moment. The child may appear to *shut down* and may curl into a defensive body position. This is often a tough judgement to make. It is highly subjective. You have to determine whether the child is experiencing the emotional distress and moving past it or whether he has become stuck in the trauma memory with no processing and no learning taking place. If the latter, then you will want to take the child down a notch. One way to do this is to instruct the child to keep his eyes open. Another is to help the child to remain grounded by reminding the child that he is in the safety of a therapy office and that the trauma memory is just a memory and that it is not happening right now (e.g., 'I realise that this is upsetting, but remember, this is just a memory...you are safe here'). You might allow the child to use the past tense. Try one of these strategies first rather than doing them all at once. Another consideration is the patient's need for support in the form of physical touch. This is a sensitive issue. It can be helpful to some children, but must be pre-empted with a question about the child's preference for physical touch (e.g., 'Would it help you if you held my hand through this?'), unless he initiates the touch. Of course, if you feel comfortable with providing physical touch at all, the physical touch should be subtle and limited to holding hands or putting your hand on the child's shoulder. Remember, some children may benefit from subtle forms of human touch, while others will become highly agitated. When you are working with young children, it is always important to consult the caregiver first about any forms of touch. Use good judgement.

11. If none of these strategies seem to do the trick, you may consider going back to a written trauma narrative and perhaps returning to Imaginal Exposure after some habituation has taken place.

12. Following the Imaginal Exposure, praise the child for the work.

    You did an amazing job. I really give you credit for trusting me and this process and having confidence in yourself that you can do this. Really nice work! [If the child is still very distressed and crying, your first priority should be to help the child to return to baseline by using a relaxation technique.]

13. Begin trauma memory processing. This typically lasts 15–20 minutes. In Prolonged Exposure this component is purposely less structured. The therapist uses open-ended questions and allows the discussion to go where the patient takes it; for example, 'Tell me how that was for you.' The goal with processing is to elicit from the child his thoughts and beliefs about the trauma and how it has influenced his life. The next chapter has more about trauma memory processing. Box 16.1 provides an example of intensive Imaginal Exposure with a 16-year-old boy with a history of sexual assault.

Background

Michael is a 16-year-old male referred to the trauma clinic by his mother due to symptoms related to a series of sexual assaults that occurred while he resided in a residential treatment facility for children and adolescents. Michael was 12 years old at the time and the perpetrator was an older adolescent who shared a room on the unit. The assaults happened over the course of Michael's first week on the unit and stopped when staff became aware of the perpetration. Michael presents with severe symptoms of PTSD and was initially highly resistant to participating in therapy where he would have to talk about the assaults.

The following is from Michael's eighth session and reflects his third session of Imaginal Exposure.

Therapist (T): What is your rating right now, Michael?

Michael (M): About a seven, I guess.

T: Okay, you can start when you're ready.

M: [Clears his throat.] It's hard to remember. I remember the first night was…it was dark. I could tell he was looking at me…or thinking about me.

T: Who?

M: This kid. Marty, I think his name was.

T: Michael, remember to tell it as though it was happening right now. Tell it in present tense.

M: Okay. He…Marty asked me… I mean, Marty asks me if I had ever done it…had sex before. I'm thinking that is kind of a strange thing to talk about when you don't know someone. [Long pause.] I'm feeling uncomfortable. I tell him I did even though I didn't. He asks me more questions…details of it and stuff. I make some stuff up. [Starts to cry.]

T: You're doing a great job, Michael. What happens next?

M: He's asking me if I've ever like done anything sexual with a guy before. I tell him no. He tells me there's nothing gay about it, that it…that guys just have sex and it's not bad in any way. He asks me if I ever thought about it. I say no.

T: You're doing great. What's your rating?

BOX 16.1 EXAMPLE DIALOGUE BETWEEN A PATIENT AND THERAPIST DURING IMAGINAL EXPOSURE

M: It's about an eight.

T: Go ahead.

M: Then I hear his bed creak and he's getting off it and coming towards my bed. I'm freaked out. Then he's right by me and I'm like terrified. He starts...he starts... [Puts his face in his hand and starts to sob.]

T: Michael, you're doing amazing. It's okay to cry through this. Remember, this is just a memory. You're safe here in this room. What happens next?

M: He puts his hand on my leg. Then he's touching me there.

T: Your penis? It's okay to say what it is.

M: Yes. I just can't move. Every part of my body is like frozen perfectly still. I'm scared to death. I don't remember him doing it but somehow he pulls my boxers down. [Sobbing.] I don't do anything about it. I'm frozen. Useless.

T: This is very brave of you, Michael. You are doing great. What is your rating now?

M: A nine.

T: What next?

M: He starts... He puts his mouth on my...penis. I feel so wrong. [Sobbing.] Just wrong! There's nothing I can do about it. I don't feel right. I don't know how long this lasted but he stops and I guess he goes to bed.

T: What do you do?

M: This is embarrassing. I don't know why this happened but...maybe being my first time or something... I don't know. I was like 12. I'm in the bathroom now and I start...masturbating. It was the first time I actually ever...you know, jerked off. It wasn't supposed to be like that.

T: You're doing good, Michael.

M: [Long pause.] He's all I can think about. I see him in my head. I can see his face and his fat head. I hate him. [Becoming angry.]

T: What's your rating, Michael?

M: I guess seven.

T: You said something happens the next day. What happens then?

BOX 16.1 CONTINUED

M: That next night he starts doing the same thing and then wants me to actually do it with him. [Starts to sob again.] It's so wrong. I'm scared. I'm not into that...but I can't say no. I'm like frozen again. He's telling me to have sex with him and tells me that's just what guys around here do.

T: You're doing good, Michael.

M: It feels so wrong. He's bending over the bed and telling me to put my... penis in him. [Sobbing.] I can't do it. Then he gets angry and turns around and grabs me. He tells me that since he sucked my dick that I have to do it to him too. [Starts to sob harder and hyperventilate.]

T: Take some deep breaths, Michael. Remember, this is only a memory. You are safe in this room. What is your rating?

M: [Long pause. Takes deep breaths.] Nine, almost ten.

T: Okay, you're doing good. What happens next?

M: So he puts it in my mouth. I'm scared to do it but scared not to. It's in there and I feel...it's disgusting. I'm choking. [Sobbing.] He's holding me. I can't get it out of my mouth. I'm choking. I could throw up. [Grabbing his abdomen.] He tells me I'm not doing it right or something. He's flipping me around. [Pause.] He's pushing me down and telling me to kneel. It's dark in the room. I'm completely frozen. I do what he says. I see the light from the small window in the door. I'm on my knees. I wish someone would come in and stop this. No one does. He's on top of me. I am trapped. I can't move. It hurts. [Sobbing.] It seems like it goes on forever. My insides hurt. I can't get away. My body...it doesn't even feel like mine anymore.

T: You are doing great, Michael. What is your rating?

M: It's just under ten.

T: Okay, go on.

M: He's finally done. He pushes away from me. I'm still frozen. It's hard for me to move. Somehow I get into the bathroom. My insides feel all messed up. They're burning. I feel like I'm bleeding there. I don't know what just happened. I don't know what to do. I go back to my bed and try to sleep but I can't.

Continues in Box 17.1

BOX 16.1 CONTINUED

CHAPTER 17
Trauma Memory Processing

In Prolonged Exposure trauma memory processing follows Imaginal Exposure. It lasts for about 15 minutes and is purposely less structured. The therapist uses open-ended questions and allows the discussion to go where the patient takes it; for example, 'Tell me how that was for you.' The goal with processing is to elicit from the child her thoughts and beliefs about the trauma and how it has influenced her life. In CPT, trauma memory processing is more structured. In particular, therapists using CPT talk about *stuck points*, or conflicting beliefs or inflexible negative beliefs related to the trauma and associated with unpleasant emotion and dysfunctional behaviour.

Stuck points can be the disagreement between a pre-trauma belief (e.g., boys who are sexually abused by men become sexual deviants) and the trauma (e.g., 'I was sexually abused by a man so will I become sexually deviant?'). In this example, if the pre-trauma belief cannot be adapted (e.g., boys who are sexually abused by men do not necessarily become sexually deviant), then the child may question his sexuality or label himself as deviant. Alternatively, the child may strongly deny that the abuse happened or try to convince himself that it was not sexual abuse. Stuck points can also be characterised by the confirmation or reinforcement of a pre-trauma negative belief (e.g., men hurt women) and the traumatic event (e.g., you are physically assaulted by a boyfriend). In this case, the child may go on to have difficult relationships with the opposite sex or adapt her behaviour to conform to this belief.

In TF-CBT, the therapist uses the written narrative to pick up on maladaptive thoughts and beliefs. Regardless of the model being used, the therapist uses Socratic dialogue and CBT techniques to identify and address pertinent themes that emerge for the child. Once a theme is identified, the therapist can explore it with the child, challenging maladaptive cognitions and helping the child to modify and adapt cognitions to reduce functional impairment. The purpose of the exercise that follows is to guide you through identifying and working with themes that emerge during trauma memory processing.

PROCESSING THE TRAUMA MEMORY

Goal

- To identify cognitive themes associated with maladaptive thoughts and functional impairment.

Procedure

1. Prepare a number of potential prompts and inquiries to facilitate processing. A number of common emerging themes are presented in Figure 17.1.

2. Encourage the child to explore and to share her perspective of the trauma: why it happened, what effect it had on the child's life, what it means for the child's future, etc.

3. It may be necessary to take a more structured approach to exploring the child's perspective by encouraging the child to respond to more specific questions; for example:

    How do you think [the trauma] has changed your reputation at school?

    How do you think [the trauma] has changed your relationship with your mum?

    How has [the trauma] changed the way you see yourself?

    Are there things about [the trauma] that are still confusing to you?

4. You may also refer to something the child may have hinted at during the therapeutic exposure; for example: 'I noticed that you had an angry tone when you talked about your father. What was your relationship like after [the trauma]?' 'You made a comment before that I wanted to ask you about. You said, "...I don't really care anymore anyway", about the way the other children treated you afterward. Tell me what you meant by that. You made a face when I said that – tell me what you think.'

5. Allow the child to assist in identifying and clarifying important themes.

    Let's pause for a moment and review some of the things we have been talking about in the past ten minutes. I wrote down some of your thoughts and comments. Let's take a look at them and see if we can come up with a common theme or story that makes sense.

6. Once you have identified a theme or a target belief, use Socratic questioning to challenge the belief or encourage the child to become more flexible in her thinking. Some possible challenge questions include the following:

    If you were asked to prove that [the belief] was true, how would you do it?

    Can you think of any other possibility, even if you don't think it is true?

    Is [the belief] 'always' true?

    Is [the belief] based on facts or based on what you hear other people say?

Abandonment. Others are unavailable or unreliable and thus unable or unwilling to provide for me or care about me.

Mistrust. Others will ultimately hurt me or take advantage of me. Everyone is out for themselves.

Shame. What happened to me has ruined my reputation and my worth as a person. I am unworthy.

Social isolation. I don't fit in. No one can understand me.

Incompetence. I can't handle things as well as others can. I can't even take care of myself. I am helpless.

Vulnerability. Something bad is going to happen to me. It is only a matter of time before I am hurt again.

No identity. I don't know who I am. I am completely defined by [mother, father, partner, the abuse, the trauma]. I don't have an identity.

Failure. I fail at everything I do. Failure for me is inevitable. I can never be as good as other people.

Entitlement. Something horrible happened to me. The world owes me everything. People need to realise this and stop making things hard for me.

Acceptance of lack of self-control. I can't control my behaviours, therefore what I do is not my fault.

Self-sacrifice. I am not worthy of good things. Let me give to others so that they can be happy.

Self-punishment. I need to be punished for what I have done. I deserve all the bad things that come my way.

Lack of self-efficacy. I can't trust my own intuition. I will follow whatever you say.

Pessimism. Life is full of disappointment. The bad outnumbers the good.

Emotional inhibition. I can't show others how I really feel.

Perfectionism. If I don't do this perfectly then I will be criticised.

FIGURE 17.1 COMMON EMERGING THEMES IN TRAUMA MEMORY PROCESSING

7. There are a number of fallible ways in which people come to conclusions or adopt certain beliefs. Whether or not you make these explicit to the child, they may help to identify which the child is using to support her maladaptive belief. Here are some examples.

> Catastrophising or blowing something out of proportion.

> Ignoring key details of a situation that challenge the belief.

> Overgeneralising the results of a single incident.

> Using emotions to confirm whether something is true.

> Misinterpreting others' behaviour to mean something it does not.

8. Box 17.1 is a continuation of Box 16.1 and provides an example of trauma memory processing with a 16-year-old boy with a history of sexual assault.

Continued from Box 16.1

Trauma memory processing

Following Imaginal Exposure the therapist encouraged Michael to reflect on the session: 'What kinds of emotions emerged? Did you remember anything you didn't think you remembered? Did you learn anything about yourself?' The therapist also targeted some specific thoughts Michael shared during the Imaginal Exposure.

Therapist (T): What was it like for you to do this, Michael?

Michael (M): It was hard... I never thought I would be able to talk about it like that...especially in detail. I'm sort of embarrassed by it but I guess I do feel like I let things off my chest a little.

T: You may feel embarrassed but there is certainly nothing to be ashamed of. And like I said before, I have heard all of this stuff before. This is not new to me. I completely understand where you are coming from. I am proud of you and the work you are doing. What kinds of emotions came up for you during the exposure?

M: More than I thought, I guess. I felt scared but also really pissed off, embarrassed and sad.

T: Good. I'm glad you recognise these. What about things that came up that surprised you?

M: Well, I always felt like guilty or like I could have done something different...like I let it happen or something. Doing this exposure I guess helped me realise how much of a victim I really was. I mean, I was only like 12. It wasn't like I was being abused now. I hardly knew anything about sex and stuff and this guy was basically an adult.

T: One thing I picked up on was that you were a bit embarrassed when you pointed out that you ended up masturbating after the first night. Tell me more about why you felt like that.

M: I felt like it was doing something wrong. I mean, why did I get like aroused and stuff when this was happening? It kind of makes sense because it was my first time and stuff... I wasn't attracted to this guy or anything.

BOX 17.1 EXAMPLE DIALOGUE BETWEEN A PATIENT AND THERAPIST DURING PROCESSING

T: You're exactly right, Michael. You getting aroused sexually had nothing to do with enjoying what was happening to you. It was simply a basic physical response that can happen to any guy when physically touched. It is very common for both boys and girls who have been sexually abused to feel like they did something wrong because at one point they may have become sexually aroused. It's just human nature. You masturbating at that time had nothing to do with the abuser. It was just normal adolescent stuff. [Pause.] What else surprised you?

M: Well, guess I never really thought I could talk about this stuff with you. I actually did it.

T: I knew you could do it and I'm glad that you were able to show yourself that you can talk about and tolerate the trauma memory. [Pause.] I also wanted to talk about what happened when your mother and father found out. From what you told me before, your mother was very supportive of you.

M: Yeah. She was.

T: It also sounded like your dad was not that supportive.

M: My dad was never really there for me. I didn't want my mother to tell him what happened...but she did. They were divorced but still talked. He didn't say anything about it to me. He acted like he didn't know. I felt like he was disgusted with me...like he thought I did something to bring it on or something.

T: Let's talk about that some more.

The therapist continues to process Michael's relationship with his father and specifically his father's response or lack of response to the sexual assault.

BOX 17.1 CONTINUED

CHAPTER 18

In-vivo Exposure

The purpose of in-vivo exposure is to improve a child's functioning by facilitating habituation to trauma associated and avoided stimuli including people, places and things in the child's life. In TF-CBT in-vivo exposure is encouraged if functional impairment is linked to avoidance strategies. For example, a child with exposure to a traumatic event in or around his school may develop an avoidance of school. In addition, a child victim of a serious car crash might develop an avoidance of travelling in vehicles.

In-vivo exposures should be discussed and arranged carefully with the caregiver, especially if the caregiver is going to function as the facilitator of the session. In-vivo exposures may or may not involve a therapist's participation. In Prolonged Exposure, in-vivo exposures are not considered an optional component of the protocol. During the initial sessions, the therapist and patient create a fear hierarchy using the distress rating scale as a means of ranking the feared stimuli. Each week the therapist and patient choose one of the feared stimuli to focus on for the in-vivo exposure exercise. Initially, a stimulus that is lower (less distressing) on the fear hierarchy is chosen in order to enable an early and relatively easy success for the patient.

PLANNING AND CONDUCTING IN-VIVO EXPOSURE

Goal

- To reduce functionally impairing avoidant behaviour in children.

Procedure

1. Explore the child's awareness of the problems associated with his avoidance of the stimuli.

   Remember when we talked about how people, places or things that were around you when [the trauma] happened may have become strongly associated with the trauma and part of the trauma memory? [Wait for response.] As [the trauma] happened near your school, is it possible that going to school now brings up memories of the trauma and makes you upset? [Wait for response.] When this happens children often start to avoid things that remind them of the trauma. They may not even know that they are doing it. In your case, school brings up [the trauma]. I am wondering if your frequent absences from school may in part be due to your avoidance of it. Your mum has mentioned that you have asked to stay home from school a lot lately because of stomach aches or headaches. Sometimes the body's way of avoiding something is to create aches and pains. What do you think? [Wait for response.] If you and I let this avoidance of school continue, what do you think will happen? [Wait for response. Use Socratic dialogue to make the point that the child will need to repeat the grade.] That's right. Too many absences or missed work will probably cause you to have to repeat the year – which it is clear you don't want to do. I want to talk to you about how we might reduce some of this avoidance and get you back to school on a regular basis.

2. Explain in-vivo exposure to the child.

   You know how we are training your body and brain not to be reactive to the trauma memory by having you think and talk about the trauma memory a lot and proving that you can be exposed to it without bad things happening? [Wait for response.] We can take the same approach with school. What I am suggesting is setting up a schedule for you to go to school with the goal of becoming very comfortable with it again. This would mean talking about what we can do to make it easier to get to school and to stay in school throughout the day. I would also like to set up a time to have you go to the school during non-school hours for about an hour. If we do this, your mum can go with you, and if it is helpful, I can go with you as well.

3. You may choose to set up a fear hierarchy specific to the feared situation whereby the exposure is conducted in a graduated manner. For example, going to the school may involve a four-step hierarchy: seeing the school from a distance (4 rating), standing in the main foyer of the school (6 rating), going to his locker (7 rating), and walking down the crowded hall in between classes (9 rating). The exposure can be structured such that at each step the child generates a distress rating and remains at that step until his ratings decrease. You may prompt for feelings and thoughts at each step. If you are not

involved in the exposure you will need to train the caregiver or whoever is the therapist (e.g., school counsellor, mentor, etc.) on the protocol.

[Therapist/facilitator] *You are doing great. Now we are going to get out of the car and walk up to the main doors of the school. We will go through the main doors and stop in the foyer. What is your rating right now?*

[Child]   *About a seven I guess.*

[Therapist/facilitator] *Okay. Let's go.* [Therapist/facilitator and child walk to school doors and enter the main foyer.] *All right, let's stand over here and take a look around. What is your rating now?*

[Child]   *Eight.*

[Therapist/facilitator] *How would you describe how you're feeling right now?*

[Child]   *Kind of nervous. It would be worse if it were crowded in here.*

[Therapist/facilitator] *What kinds of thoughts are going through your head?*

[Child]   *Um. Well, I'm sort of thinking about when it happened. That day before I went to my locker and got cornered by them in the hall. I guess my head is telling me not to go any further.*

[Therapist/facilitator] *So, that is your reactive thought. What is your proactive thought?*

[Child]   *Well, knowing what you told me and what we've been working on I guess it's that the memory of the assault is just a memory and that this is a safe place again for me. The kids that did it are gone. I guess I'm talking myself into it in a way.*

[Therapist/facilitator] *Excellent. What is your rating now?*

[Child]   *It's back to seven.*

[Therapist/facilitator] *You're doing great. Let's go a little further.*

4. Following the exposure, you should debrief the experience with the child. If you are not the facilitator, you should also debrief the exposure at the next therapy session. Like processing the trauma memory, this is where the child will process the in-vivo exposure – 'What was it like? Did you learn something about yourself? Did anything surprise you about the experience?' If you kept track of the distress ratings, you can plot them and illustrate habituation within and between steps (see Figure 18.1).

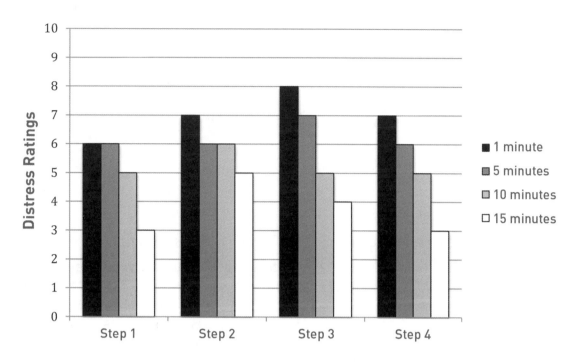

FIGURE 18.1 TRACKING AND PLOTTING DISTRESS RATINGS DURING IN-VIVO EXPOSURE

SETTING UP A FEAR HIERARCHY FOR OLDER CHILDREN AND ADOLESCENTS

Goals

- To identify functionally impairing avoidant behaviour.
- To rank avoided stimuli from most to least distressing.

Procedure

1. Copy the worksheet 'Fear Hierarchy'.

2. Explain the purpose of constructing the 'Fear (or in-vivo) Hierarchy'.

   Our primary goal today is to come up with a way to measure your level of distress or how upset you feel. The reason we want to do this is so that we can start to make a list of things in your life that you are avoiding because of the trauma. What do we typically use to measure things? [Let child respond.] Right, something with numbers. So, first we want to figure out what number corresponds to the lowest possible measurement and what number corresponds to the highest possible measurement. Typically people do 0–10, but you can also use 0–100. We will use them in the same way. [It is probably best to use 0–10 for younger or less mature children and adolescents.] Okay, so we will use 0–10. Let's take a look at this worksheet. [Worksheet 'Fear Hierarchy'.] So the lowest rating, 0, will indicate no distress or discomfort at all – complete relaxation. A rating of 10 will indicate extreme distress, or the most discomfort you felt in your entire life. Oftentimes, this is the trauma experience itself.

3. Help the child to identify anchor points at 0, 5 and 10. You can also choose to use 0–100, as is done in Prolonged Exposure.

   So, if 0 means that you are completely relaxed with no distress at all, what kinds of things would be rated a 0? [Let child respond.] Good. So, playing a videogame in bed would be a 0 for you. Let's put that down on the scale. What else? [Let child respond.] Excellent, let's put those down too. Now, what kinds of things would be rated a 10? [Let child respond.] Okay. That's what most children say. The trauma itself is the highest rating for you. Now, what things would be rated a 5? That's a little trickier because that is halfway between completely relaxed and completely distressed – somewhat distressed. What do you think? [Let child respond.] Okay. Riding the bus to school in the morning would be about a 5 for you. Doing your homework is about a 5.

4. Present the rationale for in-vivo exposure.

   Now let's talk about how we can use this to measure your level of distress to certain situations that you might be avoiding because of the trauma memory. Remember, it is common for children to want to escape or avoid situations that remind them of the trauma. Sometimes escaping or avoiding these situations is problematic and gets in the way of doing things that you have to do – such as school, getting along with people and doing fun things you used to like to do. One of the goals of this programme is to help you to confront these situations rather than to avoid them. We will do this using something called in-vivo exposure. In-vivo means 'in real life'.

For example, let's say that you have been avoiding hanging out with your friends because doing so makes you feel afraid that [the trauma] will happen again even though you know that it is unlikely that it will happen again. Your friend calls up and invites you to go to see a film at the cinema. You want to go, but you also feel a burst of anxiety because you are reminded of your fear that [the trauma] will happen again. You tell your friend that you aren't feeling up to it and immediately feel better because your anxiety decreases. However, you're also somewhat disappointed because you like going to see films with friends. Every time you reduce your anxiety by avoiding a situation, your habit of avoiding becomes stronger.

We want to reverse that habit and stop giving in to it. If you teach yourself to confront these situations rather than to avoid them and you find out that nothing bad happens, your brain learns that these situations are actually safe and that there is no need to avoid them any more.

Children with PTSD often believe that if they stay in a situation that makes them feel anxious or fearful, that their distress will get worse and worse. This is actually not the case. If you challenge yourself to stay in these situations long enough, you find that your anxiety actually lessens. Once again, this process is called habituation.

Confronting these situations will make you feel stronger and better able to handle times when you feel anxious or uncomfortable. You will learn that you are indeed able to cope with stress and you will get back to doing things rather than avoiding them.

5. Explain the in-vivo exposure instructions.

   The way in-vivo exposure works is that we come up with a list of things that you have been avoiding because of the trauma. These situations will be safe situations. It would not make sense to do this with unsafe situations. We will start with easier situations – or those that you avoid less often or less strongly. The exposure will involve confronting these situations for a period of time each week.

   Here is an example. Let's say that a child who used to love to swim has a friend who drowned in the pool. Let's say that the child tried to save his friend and was unable to do so. The situation was traumatic for him and the child started to avoid going in water – something he used to love to do. In-vivo exposure might involve the child going into the pool a little each week. Maybe the first week he simply sits at the edge of the pool and puts his feet in for 15 minutes. Then, the next week the child goes into the pool up to his waist for 15 minutes. Then, he goes in up to his neck for 15 minutes. Then, the child actually swims into the deep end of the pool for 15 minutes. Then he does this for longer and longer periods of time until the child is no longer avoidant of swimming. Does this make sense to you? [Allow child to respond. This can be a difficult concept for some children and adolescents to grasp. It may be necessary to explain using several examples or to explain in different ways.]

6. Use the hierarchy to help develop a list of situations that the child is avoiding, placing it on the hierarchy according to the intensity of distress he experiences when he imagines

confronting these situations. It is important to choose situations that are relatively safe and low-risk. Always obtain caregiver permission for the child to engage in these situations before assigning them to the child. You may need to inquire additional information from the child and parent to determine whether the situation is adequately low-risk. For example, if going to a certain park is something the child puts on the list and you are unfamiliar with the park, you will want to determine whether it is in a high crime area, how close it is to the child's house, etc.

FIGURE 18.2 EXAMPLE OF A FEAR HIERARCHY FOR A CHILD WHO EXPERIENCED A WATER-RELATED TRAUMA AND IS AVOIDANT OF SWIMMING IN POOLS

7. If the child has difficulty thinking of situations he is avoiding, you might suggest situations commonly avoided by children (see Figure 18.3). It may be helpful to first discuss possible avoided situations with the caregiver or to include the caregiver in part of the session with the child.

Being in close proximity with someone who shares certain characteristics of the perpetrator including race, gender, build, facial features, tone of voice, smell, style of clothing, profession, etc.

Someone standing in the child's personal space or approaching fast.

Human contact (e.g., touch on shoulder, hand shake, tap).

Performing the same task or activity as he did during the trauma situation.

Walking through a crowd of people.

Being out in the open.

Being alone at home or somewhere else.

Talking to unknown individuals.

Talking with someone about the trauma situation.

Being close in proximity to where the trauma occurred (e.g., school, neighbourhood).

Hugging or engaging in physical affection with family or significant others.

Showering/bathing or exposure to own sexual body parts for children who have experienced sexual abuse/assault.

Going to the doctor's office for a well child visit.

Using public toilets.

Experiencing similar bodily sensations as he felt during the trauma.

FIGURE 18.3 COMMONLY AVOIDED SITUATIONS AMONG OLDER CHILDREN AND ADOLESCENTS WITH PTSD

8. Assign the in-vivo exposure work. Begin with situations on the list rated at about 4 or lower on a 0–10 scale. Make the instructions explicit and write them down for the child. You might put the instructions on an index card. Depending on the child, you may or may not request that he records ratings of distress during the in-vivo exposure. For older adolescents it can be helpful to track distress ratings so as to illustrate that the anxiety is decreasing over the course of the exposure. Again, make sure the caregiver is on board with the assignment. Also, discuss with the caregiver and child whether it makes sense for you also to be present. For highly avoidant children, it may be helpful to provide them with on-site coaching. However, the caregiver may also be able to take on this role. See Figure 18.4 for an example of written instructions related to the pool scenario.

Tell your caregiver when you are ready to do the in-vivo exposure.

Make sure your caregiver is observing you in the pool.

Sit on the edge of the pool at the 3-foot mark and put your feet in.

At first, you may feel quite anxious. Your heart may beat faster. You may feel sick to your stomach. You may want to leave the situation immediately. Remember, that in order for this to work you must remain with your feet in the pool for 15 minutes.

Notice what your distress rating is. Does it match the rating you had on the fear hierarchy, which was about a 3?

Your anxiety will start to decrease. You may still be anxious, but you will be able to handle it.

During the 15 minutes, notice what is going on around you. What do you see? What sounds do you hear? What do you smell?

During the 15 minutes, notice how you feel and what thoughts are entering your mind.

Notice how the water feels on your skin.

About halfway into the exposure, check on your distress rating. Is it the same as when you started? Has it decreased?

Check on your distress rating again at the end of the exposure. Has it decreased? Notice how you feel and what thoughts are entering your mind. Have these changed?

Tell your caregiver when you are done.

Give yourself credit for doing the exposure. You should feel good about yourself.

FIGURE 18.4 EXAMPLE OF WRITTEN IN-VIVO EXPOSURE INSTRUCTIONS

9. Review the in-vivo exposure at the next session. Examine and discuss the distress ratings across the exposure period, as well as the child's observations (i.e., sights, sounds, smells) and feelings and thoughts during the exposure.

PART 4

Working with the Caregiver

CHAPTER 19

What Does the Caregiver Bring to the Table?

Establishing a collaborative working relationship with caregivers and engaging them in their children's treatment begins at first contact and remains critical throughout treatment. Unlike adults, children and adolescents are dependent on caregivers and their continuation in treatment is contingent on whether the caregiver believes that the treatment will benefit her child enough to offset the sacrifices made to commit to a treatment protocol and the emotional burden associated with talking about the trauma. Parental *buy-in* has been significantly associated with treatment compliance and engagement (McKay *et al.* 2004). Further, children with caregivers who do not buy into the child's therapy and show little engagement in their child's treatment often perceive their caregiver's lack of commitment, and this may influence their ability to commit and engage in treatment. In contrast, caregivers who show an active interest and engagement in their child's therapy engender a sense of hope and support. The rationale for exposure often sounds paradoxical to caregivers, and many of them require ongoing reassurance that this strategy is effective in the long term, despite the possibility that the child may experience a resurgence of symptoms or trauma reminders in the short term. Thus, it is critical to engage caregivers early on and to help them to understand the rationale behind the therapeutic approach and to feel encouraged to actively participate in and contribute to their child's therapy.

There are a number of things that can get in the way of a caregiver's positive engagement in their child's therapy. First, caregivers may place blame on themselves for the child having been exposed to trauma and for the subsequent consequences. Consider the case of a victim of intimate partner violence who feels she did not adequately protect her child from the violence, perceives the child as blaming her, and therefore avoids discussing the violence with her child.

Second, caregivers may be so overwhelmed with a number of other life stressors that they are emotionally unavailable to support the child in therapy. In fact, they may not even realise their lack of support of the child. Research suggests that a greater number of parental stressors and increased parental distress are associated with increased severity of children's traumatic stress (Kelley *et al.* 2010; Morris, Gabert-Quillen and Delahanty 2012; Roberts *et al.* 2012).

Third, caregivers with a history of trauma may have unaddressed trauma-related symptoms of their own and may tend to avoid or distance themselves from their child's trauma exposure. In fact, the child's trauma exposure may cause some of their own trauma-related issues to resurface, exacerbating emotional and behavioural problems and compromising parenting. The intergenerational nature of PTSD was recently highlighted in a large study of women and their children, demonstrating that children of mothers with a history of trauma and a PTSD diagnosis were more likely than children with mothers without PTSD to be exposed to trauma and to develop traumatic stress (Roberts *et al.* 2012).

Fourth, some caregivers may become so preoccupied with the child's disruptive behaviour problems that they lose sight of the child's emotional struggle with the trauma. These caregivers may even resent that the therapist is focusing mainly on the child's trauma exposure, feeling that more effort should be placed on reducing the child's disruptive or aggressive behaviours.

Finally, some children are living with temporary or unfamiliar caregivers at the time of their treatment. Although many foster and relative caregivers play active and supportive roles in their children's treatment, some feel it is not their responsibility to participate in therapy with the children in their care, particularly in a system in which they share no legal authority over the children. In fact, foster parents are commonly not apprised of their foster children's history of abuse and trauma.

To this end, one of the first steps in therapy is to gather information about the caregiver and their relationship with the child and connection to the child's trauma. This information will help you to better conceptualise how the caregiver and family fit into the child's presentation of symptoms and will help to establish a more informed treatment approach. The Baseline Trauma Interview provides an outline of the kinds of information that may be useful to obtain from caregivers. The following exercises show how to refer caregivers to their own treatment, should it be warranted.

BASELINE CAREGIVER INTERVIEW

Goals

- To obtain information from the caregiver that will inform case conceptualisation and treatment planning.
- To identify potential barriers to treatment and to parental engagement in treatment.

Procedure

1. Use the worksheet 'Baseline Caregiver Interview'.

2. Explain to the caregiver the reason for collecting information about him and his relationship with the child.

   Today I would like to find out more about you and your relationship with your child. Too often, we therapists do not know enough about caregivers really to optimise their ability to help their children succeed in therapy. We simply don't ask the right questions. I do not want to make that mistake and would like to go through a list of questions that will help to provide me with information to better design our approach to helping your child. Some of the questions are personal and have to do with your past experiences and others have to do with your relationship with your child. How do you feel about this? [Wait for caregiver to respond and discuss any concerns or questions.]

3. Conduct a semi-structured interview addressing the domains outlined in the worksheet 'Baseline Caregiver Interview'. Feel free to add questions to the interview based on the child's situation and your preliminary conceptualisation of the case.

   Thank you for agreeing to this. This will be an important piece of your [son/daughter's] treatment. If there is anything that I ask that you do not feel comfortable talking about, please let me know and I will respect your wishes.

REFERRING THE CAREGIVER TO TREATMENT

Goals

- To explore the caregiver's willingness to seek professional help for her own mental health problems or problems related to the child's trauma.

- To educate the caregiver on how mental health problems and trauma-related symptoms, including from the child's trauma, can negatively impact on parenting and the parent's ability to support the child.

- To make an informed referral, should the caregiver request one.

Procedure

1. Review the worksheet 'Baseline Caregiver Interview'.

2. Provide the handout 'What Can Get in the Way of a Caregiver's Ability to Support the Traumatised Child?'

3. Review findings from the 'Baseline Caregiver Interview' worksheet suggesting that the caregiver could benefit from her own mental health services.

   I wanted to revisit some of our discussion from last time regarding how your child's trauma has affected you. In the course of the interview you brought up your own lifelong battle with depression and your tendency towards alcoholism. You said that depression has been something that has been in and out of your life now since you were a child and that it had been relatively good for a while, but came back strong after you learned of your child's trauma. You also told me that you tend to drink more when you are depressed and that lately you have found yourself drinking more than you should. It sounds like you received some counselling in the past and that it seemed to help you. You've also been on antidepressants in the past and they also seemed to help.

   It is not uncommon for a child's trauma exposure to worsen existing feelings of depression and anxiety in caregivers. In fact, a child's trauma exposure can be potentially traumatic to the parent and lead to trauma-related symptoms and PTSD. This makes it very hard for caregivers to help their child. You've heard the saying, 'You have to help yourself before you can help others'. It's like when parents are told to put the oxygen masks on first in the event of a plane malfunction so that they are conscious and able to put the mask on their child.

4. Explain that the caregiver attending to her own mental health needs will greatly help the child succeed in treatment. Review the handout 'What Can Get in the Way of a Caregiver's Ability to Support the Traumatised Child?'

   You have a challenging task ahead of you. Much of children's success in treatment is owed to caregivers. A lot of the work we do in therapy sessions is only effective if it is applied outside of therapy: at home and elsewhere. I rely a lot on caregivers to be able to help bring this material home – literally and figuratively. However, depression, anxiety, PTSD and addiction can easily get in the way of a caregiver's ability to do that.

Caregivers are models for their children on how to manage and cope with intense emotions and respond to stress adaptively. In addition, caregiver support is crucial to children who are undergoing trauma-focused treatment. How do you feel about getting involved in your own treatment?

5. Discuss possible treatment options for the caregiver, or if the target problem is not clear, encourage the caregiver to seek a comprehensive mental health assessment. Make an informed referral.

ENGAGING THE CAREGIVER IN THE CHILD'S TREATMENT

Goals

- To emphasise the importance of caregiver engagement in the child's treatment.
- To discuss the role of the caregiver in the child's treatment.

Procedure

1. Provide the handout 'Why Caregiver Involvement is Critical to Child Trauma Treatment'.

2. Explain and emphasise the importance of caregiver involvement in treating child traumatic stress.

   A good deal of research on how effective treatment is in reducing children's traumatic stress has determined that treatment outcomes are better when a caregiver is actively involved in the treatment. I want to discuss with you what this means and talk about what you can do to make this programme the most effective for your child.

3. Explain the importance of getting the child to treatment on a regular basis.

   The first thing is kind of a no-brainer – children who get to therapy sessions on a regular basis do better than children who skip a lot of sessions or discontinue treatment early. There are a lot of factors that go into making it to treatment on time and on a regular basis. Sometimes traffic is bad. Things do indeed happen that get in the way of making it to a treatment session. So long as it doesn't happen again and again, one or two missed sessions won't matter much. However, I have seen children who end up missing just about every other session or come to a session two or three times and then go two or three weeks without coming to a session. When therapy is inconsistent, especially trauma-focused therapy, progress may suffer. In this programme, each component informs the next. That means that information we go over at one session is mastered in order to go on to the next. If there is a long interval between sessions, the information doesn't always carry forward.

4. Discuss caregiver praise and encouragement.

   Trauma treatment is challenging for children. Another way that caregivers play a supportive role is by regularly praising and providing encouragement to their children throughout the course of therapy. Praise and encouragement should happen after every session. It is better if it's not generic praise, but specific to something the child did. For example, some children may get praise simply for agreeing to come and tolerate therapy. These children may not do too much in session – but they are at least present. Other children may excel at a certain skill-building exercise or express themselves particularly well in a session and deserve praise specific to that. I will always let you know what your child did well in session. Other sources of praise can happen at home. If you observe your child implementing something we went over in therapy at home, be keen to point that out and praise the child. Even when there is unwanted behaviour happening at home, look for the 'praise-able' behaviour.

5. Discuss the role of caregivers in modelling healthy emotion regulation and stress management at home.

   Children are much more likely to learn and adopt certain skills if they see other people doing it at home. Caregivers are key role models for children, even when it doesn't seem like their children are paying much attention to them. If a caregiver is using the skill, then the child is more likely to apply it outside of therapy. In the course of therapy, we will go over several skills focused on better managing intense emotion, problem solving and responding to stress in healthy ways. You and I will also go over whatever I work on with the child. If you make a concerted effort to practise these outside of session, then your child will surely notice this.

6. Discuss caregiver participation in conjoint sessions.

   There may be times when I request that you and your child come together in session for a skill-building exercise, to discuss an issue that has come up or to discuss the trauma memory. My hope is that during this time you feel comfortable enough really to engage in the session and confident enough to assist me in teaching the skill to your child, facing the issue head on, or discussing the trauma memory.

7. Discuss the caregiver's role in enhancing caregiver, child and family social and personal resources.

   Trauma can take a toll on children and families – including caregivers. Often, certain child, caregiver and family resources are spent or exhausted dealing with the aftermath of the trauma. It is important that these resources are replaced or enhanced. This takes a concerted effort. By resources I mean social support for you, your child and the family, protected family time and sources of advocacy and support, among other things. Caregivers should be taking a mental needs assessment of themselves, their children and the family – filling in gaps where indicated.

8. Discuss caregivers' ability to face their own past and their own personal issues.

   Even though this therapy is for your child, your involvement in the therapy will likely bring up personal issues for you – and may even elicit memories of painful experiences from the past, including potential trauma. Some caregivers are highly resistant to these, while others are open to examining them as they come up and as they relate to the child or the parent–child relationship. In addition, sometimes there is enough that comes up that it makes sense for caregivers to arrange for their own therapy or treatment.

9. Discuss the caregiver's reactions to the trauma memory.

   As the child progresses through the programme she will become less and less emotionally distressed when talking about the trauma. This is because we are training the body and brain to be less reactive to the trauma memory and to identify it as just that – a memory. It is the expectation that this will also happen for the caregiver. It can be highly upsetting for caregivers to remember terrible things that happened to their children – especially when it includes detailed information. If a caregiver continues to respond to the trauma memory by becoming visibly upset in front of the child, even after the child no longer responds with this level of distress, then she may get a mixed message that maybe she should be as upset as her caregiver – or that she is somehow undermining her caregiver.

CHAPTER 20

What is Trauma and How Does it Affect My Child?

Caregivers often come to therapy with a lot of questions about how trauma exposure has affected their children and what can be done about it. Sometimes they are misinformed with myths about trauma exposure in children and/or child development more generally. These can be scary. For example, consider a caregiver who thinks that his child's sexual abuse will result in him exhibiting sexually deviant behaviour as an adult. Like the psychoeducation component for children, the psychoeducation component for caregivers should cover all of the material provided to children, as well as additional information specific to caregivers. The following exercises are designed to facilitate this component.

WHAT IS CHILD TRAUMATIC STRESS?

Goals

- To educate the caregiver on how trauma is defined.
- To educate the caregiver of common indicators of traumatic stress.

Procedure

1. Provide the handout 'A Caregiver's Introduction to Child Traumatic Stress'.

2. Explain that a number of different types of extremely stressful events can be traumatic.

   Child traumatic stress is a psychological response to an extremely stressful event characterised by a host of emotional and behavioural problems. A number of different types of events can be traumatic including what is considered non-interpersonal or unintentional types of trauma, such as serious accidents and natural disasters, as well as interpersonal or intentionally violent types of trauma, such as child physical or sexual abuse, community violence and war exposure. The diagnostic classification systems used to diagnose PTSD define trauma as exposure to death or threatened death, serious injury or illness, or sexual violence such that one has directly experienced, witnessed it happening to someone else, learned that something violent or accidental happened to a loved one or someone close, or experienced repeated exposure to details of the event.

3. Explain that child traumatic stress can interfere with a child's normal functioning.

   Left untreated, child traumatic stress can lead to problems in a child's day-to-day functioning at school, at home and with friends. One way to think about what is going on is at the level of the brain. In truly threatening or dangerous situations, our brain signals to us that there is an emergency. Our systems go on 'red alert'. This red alert system relies on an 'autopilot' programme that enables us to respond to the danger in adaptive ways. For example, if we are faced with a dangerous wild animal, we need to respond rapidly in order to get away or fight back. If we think too hard about it or try to 'problem solve' in the ordinary way, we would not be able to respond quickly enough. So this 'autopilot' programme actually turns down our ability to 'problem solve' and enables us simply to respond. Traumatic stress is kind of like if the brain continued to operate on 'autopilot' even after the danger was gone. This means that our ability to problem solve and think through situations is compromised, while our stress response system is ramped up. You can imagine the difficulty a child might have in school, for example, if he was operating in this mode.

4. Explain common symptoms of traumatic stress.

   Common symptoms of traumatic stress include having upsetting images or thoughts of what happened come into mind, nightmares, having strong physical and emotional responses to reminders of the trauma as well as normal day-to-day stressors, having difficulty distinguishing between relatively safe situations and dangerous situations, overreacting to daily challenges, avoiding people, places, things or situations that remind us of what happened, operating on 'high alert', having trouble sleeping, easily becoming irritable or aggressive, having trouble concentrating or paying attention, having physical symptoms such as aches and pains, having mood and thought processes that have become more negative, relationship problems and increased risky or disruptive behaviour. Children and adolescents can also develop a deep sense of shame associated with the trauma.

5. Discuss children and adolescents' reactions to traumatic stress.

   Having traumatic stress reactions can be confusing and degrading for children and adolescents. They may interpret these behaviours as being childlike or immature. They may become embarrassed or self-conscious about their responses to stress and their bodily responses to trauma reminders. They may feel stigmatised and as though they are the only ones with these problems – leading to social isolation. Some children and adolescents may display extreme avoidant behaviour that holds them back from having developmentally normal experiences, while others may engage in high-risk or reckless behaviour that puts themselves or others in danger. Adolescents may also turn to alcohol and/or drugs to escape from traumatic stress and feelings of isolation.

CHAPTER 21

How Will Psychotherapy Help My Child?

Describing the components of the therapy model and explaining the rationale of the treatment approach to the caregiver is critical in earning the caregiver's trust and recruiting her to be a member of your team. Caregivers may or may not have had any experience with psychotherapy, and if they have, it may have been a non-validated approach or one with potential for harm (e.g. Holding Therapy; Lilienfeld 2007). It is also important for the caregiver to have an overall understanding of the mechanisms behind these components in order to *bring home* principles of the recovery plan and to help to extend what is learned in therapy sessions to other aspects of the child's life (i.e., home, school, community). The caregiver does not need to become an expert on psychotherapy; she simply needs to understand the basic elements of the treatment approach.

Many of the caregivers you work with may not have a strong educational background. A useful approach to teaching complex or abstract concepts is to use analogies. Analogies can provide caregivers with a tangible representation of the psychological phenomenon at hand. In addition, it is a good idea to provide caregivers with printed materials that they can reference at home. Information provided in initial sessions can be overwhelming for a caregiver. Providing additional (albeit light) reading will allow the caregiver to review the material on her own time and may prevent her from seeking information from the internet or other places that may or may not come from reputable sources. In fact, much of the information available online is misrepresented and potentially contrary to what you are trying to convey.

WHAT WORKS AND HOW?

Goals

- To provide caregivers with a basic overall understanding of *what works* in treating child traumatic stress and *how*.

- To gain credibility and to establish a working relationship with the caregiver.

Procedure

1. Provide the handout 'How Trauma Treatment Works: For Caregivers'.

2. Explain evidence-based approaches to treating child traumatic stress.

   Based on years of research, the treatment approach with the most evidence of effectiveness for treating child traumatic stress involves therapeutic exposure and trauma memory processing. These are key components in a number of evidence-based therapies including TF-CBT and Prolonged Exposure. In fact, these are the principal components of all psychotherapy for anxiety disorders in children and adolescents. Although there will always be children and adolescents who do not respond to certain treatments, exposure-based therapy is so far the one with the best evidence to support it.

3. Provide an explanation of the basic mechanisms of exposure-based treatment.

   Therapeutic exposure is where we help the child or adolescent revisit the trauma memory in detail, either by writing a narrative about it or by narrating it out loud. What we are looking to do is called habituation. We want to train the body and brain not to react to the trauma memory as though it is an actual threat. This happens by literally showing the body and brain that it can be exposed to the memory without something bad happening. Imagine that you have an intense fear of bridges, meaning that bridges cause you significant distress. Now imagine that you move to an area where you have to cross a bridge, or multiple bridges, to get to work. Therapeutic exposure would involve slowly exposing you to bridges until you are able to cross the bridge multiple times. First I might show you a picture of a bridge. Next I might ask you to watch a video of cars going over a bridge. Then, I might have you look at the bridge from a distance. Over time we get closer and closer to the bridge until you are going over it again and again. Every time you increase the intensity of the exposure, you feel uncomfortable and anxious. Over the course of each exposure, however, your body starts to relax and you realise that nothing bad is happening. You habituate. As sessions continue, you are habituating within session, as well as between sessions. This is the same as therapeutic exposure to the trauma memory, only the trauma memory is not something we can look at, but something we have to draw up through visualisation or narration. [Explain to the caregiver the protocol you will be using with her child.]

   Let me use a different analogy to explain trauma memory processing. I have a cupboard at home where I throw all kinds of things that I don't really know what to do with – tonnes of shoes and other things that I just toss in there. It is disorganised and full of stuff. Imagine that the 'stuff' is pieces of the trauma memory. For children, the trauma memory is often fragmented in a bunch of pieces and disorganised. The child tries hard to avoid these pieces and tosses them away – into the cupboard. Now, imagine it becoming so full of these fragments that every now and then, the cupboard door just opens up on its own and all these pieces come tumbling out. Imagine that this happens at the most inconvenient times – such as when you have guests over. Therapy involves opening up the cupboard, taking all of the little pieces of the trauma memory out, laying them out on the floor, putting them in order and into neat piles, and then returning them to the cupboard in an organised fashion. Afterwards, the trauma memory is intact and cohesive. It is stored so that the door can close and stay closed, and so that you can go into the cupboard and refer to the trauma memory when you need to. So, the child gains control of the trauma memory and starts to make sense of the trauma in the context of her life.

CHAPTER 22
Bringing it Home

Therapy happens one hour a week at best. This means that most of the work being done is happening outside of therapy. The point here is that therapeutic exposure does not end in the therapy session. In fact, child-initiated discussions about the trauma increase in frequency and duration during the therapeutic exposure phase of treatment (Grasso, Joselow, *et al.* 2011). Caregivers report that these discussions seem to happen at random times and are often short-lived, consisting of a statement made by the child about the trauma followed by the start of a different topic. These are important and reflect that the child is continuing to process the trauma memory at home. Caregivers should be encouraged to listen to the child and provide support.

There is much data in non-human animals supporting the re-emergence of a conditioned fear association following extinction when animals are placed in a different context (Vervliet, Craske and Hermans 2013). For example, if you pair a light with a shock in a metal cage so that the animal responds to the light as it did to the shock, it will present this same behaviour if placed in a different context – let's say a plastic container. If the animal undergoes extinction learning in the new context, it will no longer show the response to the light. However, if the animal is then returned to the original context (i.e., the metal cage), there is a high likelihood that the learned association will re-emerge. Thus, the learning is context-dependent.

Although there has been little research into this phenomenon in human patients with PTSD, the basic behavioural pattern makes sense and suggests the potential advantage of undergoing therapeutic exposure in multiple contexts, especially at home. The increase in child and caregiver discussion of trauma at home during the exposure phase of treatment may be an indication that some of this is happening naturally. However, you might consider encouraging the caregiver to initiate some of these discussions with the caveat that the caregiver should be deemed prepared to facilitate such discussions in a therapeutic manner. There is currently no research available on this. In adult treatment of PTSD, though, participating in a therapeutic exposure exercise at home is part of the protocol. In Prolonged Exposure, adult patients are instructed to bring home a recording of the session and to listen to it three or more times during the week while recording distress ratings. These are separate from in-vivo exposure exercises. In CPT, adult patients are instructed to complete home writing assignments pertaining to trauma material. While TF-CBT does not include such a task, you might think about ways in which you can implement supplemental exercises to be done in different contexts of the child's life. As always, doing so necessitates oversight by the caregiver.

TALKING TO YOUR CHILD ABOUT THE TRAUMA

Goals

- To teach caregivers to engage in healthy discussion about the trauma in response to the child's prompts.

Procedure

1. Provide the handout 'How to Talk to Your Children about Trauma'.

2. Teach the caregiver to recognise and take advantage of opportunities to talk to their child about the trauma.

   You can help your child to better process emotions and thoughts related to the trauma by being receptive to his attempts to talk about the trauma outside of therapy sessions. Facilitating trauma-related discussion at home provides your child with more opportunities to better understand what happened and to make sense of how it fits into his life.

3. Review the guidelines (also on the handout) on how to facilitate a therapeutically beneficial conversation about the trauma.

4. Explore your personal feelings about your child's trauma exposure. Anticipate your reactions and think about how they may affect your child. You might do this by sharing your feelings with other adults or professionals, or by writing in a journal.

5. Catch yourself when you attempt to avoid talking about the child's trauma. Work on reducing avoidance of trauma-related discussion and show your child that you are willing to talk openly about it.

6. Encourage trauma-related discussion gradually. For example, you might start with discussions that are more general (e.g., how someone *else* who experienced sexual abuse might feel), slowly moving towards discussion about the child's personal experience (e.g., how the child feels about being sexually abused).

7. Sometimes caregivers ask questions that unintentionally encourage children to feel as if they did something wrong. To avoid encouraging feelings of shame or self-blame, ask questions in ways that are supportive. For example, instead of saying, 'Why didn't you tell me sooner?', you might say, 'What made you decide to tell me when you did?'

8. Use open-ended questions. Questions that are phrased to elicit one-word responses often end with the one-word response. Therapists are trained to ask questions that necessitate more involved responses. For example, instead of saying, 'Do you feel like you have a better understanding of what happened that day?', you might say, 'You've done a lot of work in therapy. How do you think working with the therapist has given you a better understanding of what happened that day?'

9. Allow the child to set the pace of the conversation. Do not pressure him to talk more than he wants to. This will discourage the child from talking in the future. When the child is finished, allow the conversation to end.

CHAPTER 23
Managing Difficult Behaviour

It is essential to include a focus on parental management of difficult behaviour, even in a therapy designed to treat child traumatic stress. For many caregivers, their child's disruptive behaviour is what is most palpable in the home and at school. It compromises family and peer relationships and often leads to disciplinary problems in school and in the community. Improper management of difficult behaviour can have negative consequences on the child's trauma treatment. First, it can impair the parent–child relationship and reduce the support that the caregiver is able to give to the child. Second, it can lead to *crises of the week* in which the child faces disciplinary issues at school or other real-life consequences of her behaviour. These can draw away from the therapy's primary focus. Further, research has demonstrated that during the exposure phase of therapy, children's behaviour may temporarily worsen (Cohen *et al.* 2006). Proper parental management of behaviour problems can provide the structure to *survive the storm* until positive growth happens.

Some children and adolescents will present with behaviour problems that require more intensive clinical attention. The developers of TF-CBT suggest incorporating a functional behaviour analysis to determine the function of the unwanted behaviour and to identify the most disruptive behaviours (Cohen, Berliner and Mannarino 2010). Other children may require a referral to programmes that specialise in behaviour management, such as Multisystemic Therapy (Henggeler 1999).

This chapter provides an introduction on conducting a functional behaviour analysis and exercises on behaviour management techniques often used in the treatment of children with traumatic stress.

A FUNCTIONAL BEHAVIOUR ANALYSIS

Goal

- To understand the function of the unwanted behaviour.

Procedure

1. Hand out the worksheet 'What is the Function of This Behaviour?'

2. Explain the basic approach to a functional behaviour analysis.

   A functional behaviour analysis is a scientific way of determining the function of behaviour. We assume that a child behaves in a certain way in order to achieve something. There is a reason behind the behaviour. This doesn't necessarily mean that the child is aware of why she is doing it. For example, a child who clowns around in class may be rewarded when other students laugh at her jokes. We call this positive reinforcement. A child who frequently feels sick to her stomach before school may be avoiding going to school because she is being bullied at school. By having a stomach ache and being allowed to stay home from school, she is negatively reinforced – able to avoid an adverse experience. We want to break behaviour down into small parts and analyse it to determine the trigger or antecedent and the consequence.

3. Introduce the 'What is the Function of This Behaviour?' worksheet.

   This is the form we will use to break the behaviour into parts and collect the data. Traditionally, a functional behaviour analysis is done by trained observers in the context of the behaviour. In other words, the behaviour is broken into its component parts and analysed in real time using direct observation. We are going to modify this approach – we're going to use this worksheet to gather observations that you have already made.

4. Break the behaviour into its component parts.

   Let's make a list of the unwanted behaviour, trying to be as specific as possible.

5. Encourage the caregiver to think about what typically happens immediately prior to the behaviour. Is there a pattern or identifiable trigger? Triggers may include others' behaviour, a certain time of day, a place or a trauma reminder.

   Let's take a look at the column that says 'What usually comes before the behaviour?' Here we want to think back to specific times when your child has shown this behaviour. Do you recognise a pattern? Is there something that happens right before the behaviour? It could be something that somebody does, something your child sees on television or a certain time of day.

6. Have the caregiver generate specific effects or consequences of the behaviour.

   Now let's look at the column that says 'What usually happens because of the behaviour?' Here we want to think about specific things that happen because of the behaviour.

7. Look for patterns and hypothesise a possible function of each of the behaviours. These may be related to the trauma and the child's traumatic stress, but they do not have to be.

With an idea about what may prompt the behaviour and what happens because of the behaviour, we can now generate some possible functions of the behaviour.

STEP ONE	STEP TWO	STEP THREE	STEP FOUR	STEP FIVE
What is the behaviour?	**What usually comes before the behaviour?**	**What usually happens because of the behaviour?**	**What is the possible function of the behaviour?**	**What can be done to alter this pattern?**
She [foster daughter] tears apart her room and pounds her fist on the wall.	Supervised visitation arranged with her younger siblings in different foster homes.	First we get upset. Then when she's calm, we try to talk to her about what's going through her head.	She is emotionally upset after visiting with her siblings and pounding on the wall and being destructive relieves some of that distress. It also gets us to pay special attention to her.	Intervene after the visit to debrief – explore her feelings and thoughts. Perhaps schedule her therapy appointment to follow the visit.

FIGURE 23.1 EXAMPLE OF DETERMINING THE FUNCTION OF A BEHAVIOUR

8. Review the possible functions and discuss ways of manipulating the context in order to change the behaviour. For example, if the reward or reinforcement is eliminated, it is likely that the behaviour will be minimised or eliminated. Likewise, if the *trigger* or antecedent of the behaviour is eliminated, so might the behaviour. Another approach is to associate the behaviour with a different consequence, one that does not function as a reward. In addition, you could implement ways of satisfying the child's need for something that is functioning as a reward or reinforcement (e.g., attention from a parent) so that the child does not have to engage in unwanted behaviour to obtain it. There are a number of possible approaches that you can discuss with the caregiver.

9. Have the caregiver prioritise which behaviours are most critical to change. Choose only *one* behaviour to focus on at a time – trying to change more than one behaviour at once can become confusing.

CATCHING THE CHILD DOING GOOD

Goal

- To encourage the caregiver actively to look for *good* behaviour and to recognise it.

Procedure

1. Provide the handout 'How to Recognise and Reinforce Improvement'.

2. Explain that behaviour need not be perfect to recognise when there is improvement.

   Change takes time. Getting from point A to point B rarely happens in a straight line. It may take children a number of small changes in behaviour before they completely achieve the behavioural goal. Recognising and praising these smaller benchmarks helps to move them along. This is because positive reinforcement is a key component of learning new behaviour.

3. Emphasise that it is sometimes difficult for caregivers to notice improvement in behaviour because they have been used to focusing on the negative behaviour.

   It can be very difficult for caregivers who are used to catching their child behaving poorly to notice subtle improvements in behaviour. The behaviour is sometimes so difficult and chronic that caregivers may begin to expect the behaviour and become sensitive to it – which means that they are quicker to detect the unwanted behaviour than positive behaviour. Sometimes improvement is simply the absence of the unwanted behaviour. If, for example, you notice that the unwanted behaviour is less frequent, it may help to reinforce this by praising the child for showing improvement.

4. Review the guidelines in the handout 'How to Recognise and Reinforce Improvement'.

5. Help the caregiver make a list of specific behaviours or signs of improvement that she could praise.

WHEN TO ACTIVELY IGNORE AND WHEN TO ACT

Goal

- To encourage caregivers to ignore unwanted but less serious behaviour.
- To encourage caregivers to be directive about potentially serious or risky behaviours.

Procedure

1. Provide the handout 'When to Actively Ignore and When to Act'.

2. Explain the rationale behind ignoring mildly unwanted behaviour.

   It seems counterintuitive to ignore negative behaviour – but sometimes it is the best thing to do. Think about it. When you are paying attention to your child's behaviour, good or bad, you are providing the child with your undivided attention. Your attention, even if it is negative, may be rewarding to your child. In other words, the very act of trying to stop the behaviour may be causing more of it to happen. If the behaviour is unwanted, but not serious, then ignoring the behaviour will remove the reward (your attention), and potentially reduce the likelihood that your child will do it next time.

3. Help the caregiver to make a list of behaviours that are unwanted but less serious or mild.

4. Teach the caregiver to be directive when faced with more disruptive behaviours without getting involved in a *power struggle*.

   What happens when your child starts to raise her voice, yell or scream? [Let caregiver respond.] Do you ever raise your voice in response? [Let caregiver respond.] Of course, that is natural, right? What does your child do in return? [Let caregiver respond.] Right, she raises her voice louder. This can go back and forth until you're both involved in a screaming match. What if a different approach was taken? What if instead of raising your voice, you lowered your voice? How do you think your child would respond? [Pause.] She would certainly have to work a little harder to hear what you are saying. She might even start to lower her voice as well. In communication, we will often lower our voice until it matches the tone of the voice of the person we are talking to. Now, lowering your voice doesn't mean you shouldn't be directive. You can be directive and firm without having to raise your voice.

5. Help the caregiver to make a list of behaviours that might elicit a firm and directive approach.

6. Provide guidelines on using consequences to change negative behaviour.

   Consequences can be effective. There are a number of things that make consequences more effective. First, always make sure the consequence is enforceable so that you can follow through with the consequence should your child continue with the behaviour. If it is not enforceable, your child may call your bluff. The consequence should be something important to your child (e.g., videogame access). Consequences should be consistent and predictable so that your child starts to make an informed decision about her behaviour. Finally, a consequence is best when it is short in duration or when there is room to apply more consequences or intensify the consequence. If you apply the worst consequence, then you have no leverage left to address subsequent behaviour.

SCORE KEEPER

Goal

- To help the caregiver to implement a reward system for behaviour change.

Procedure

1. Refer to the worksheet 'The Score Keeper'.

2. Introduce the score keeper method.

   It is typical for older children and adolescents to scoff at point systems and token economy-style interventions. However, if it doesn't look like your average star chart, they might actually take to it. Indeed, we all use reward systems. Think about the coffee card. I am constantly getting a free coffee with every ten purchased. I have had success implementing a reward system to reinforce behaviour change in adolescents by borrowing from the coffee card idea. It is simple. The child or adolescent keeps a wallet-sized card at hand and the caregiver initials the card when the desired behaviour is presented.

3. Work with the child and caregiver together to create a list of behaviours worthy of earning points.

4. Create a list of rewards with different point values. For example, the child might turn in 5 points in order to add 15 minutes to her curfew or the child might turn in 15 points to eat at a desired restaurant.

5. Explain that the child is responsible for keeping track of the card and that if the card is lost, the points are lost. The approach can also be designed such that it is the child's responsibility to alert the caregiver when she exhibits the desired behaviour. This encourages the child to pay attention to her behaviour and to self-monitor.

6. Another option is to include the desired behaviours on the card to function as a reminder to the child.

CHAPTER 24

Engaging Families with Barriers to Treatment

Engaging and maintaining families poses serious challenges for all outpatient mental health providers. A significant portion of children identified as in need of treatment are lost before they even make it to intake (Watt and Dadds 2007). In general, about one-fifth of all child and adolescent outpatient mental health intakes and about a third of all subsequent sessions are missed (Watt and Dadds 2007). This is also true for children coming into trauma-focused therapy (Bryant *et al.* 2007). Some data suggests that among patients who remain in treatment, those with better attendance show better treatment outcomes (Farmer *et al.* 2003; Kazdin and Kendall 1998).

Children most at-risk for dropping out of treatment or having low attendance tend to exhibit more severe symptomatology, live in low-income families, experience greater family stress and dysfunction and have caregivers with mental health issues or high levels of perceived stress (Snell-Johns, Mendez and Smith 2004). These families are often juggling numerous challenges including partner conflict, poverty, crime, poor school systems, teenage pregnancy and substance misuse. They often operate in a chronic crisis mode – when one fire is put out, another flames up. Clearly, these are families with tremendous challenges and steep barriers to treatment.

The reasons for dropout and missed appointments are multifold. Transportation is often an issue. Even when public transportation is available, it is often too costly for the family, or requires a significant amount of travel time. Childcare is also problematic. It is not unusual to have a family comprised of a single mother and several children. The mother's need to attend to all of her children often prohibits her from meeting the traumatised child's needs. Many of these families are in need of basic services that extend the scope of what mental health treatment typically provides. Overcoming these barriers may require you to collaborate with the family on finding solutions. It is often helpful for you to visit the family in their own environment. Observing the family at home can be very telling. Obstacles may become clearer, as well as strategies to overcome them. Being flexible depends on your willingness to extend your services to address family factors that are getting in the way of the child's treatment. This could mean forming collaborations with other family members, helping the family to find a reliable means of transportation, working with the school system or providing therapy at home or in the family's community.

In a recent survey of providers' strategies for engaging families in treatment, Watt and Dadds (2007) identified two approaches: *structural strategies*, or attending to and minimising practical obstacles, and *process strategies*, or those relating to motivation and/or the family–therapist relationship. Structural strategies may include (a) providing childcare during sessions; (b) facilitating transportation arrangements either via medical transport or fare reimbursement; (c) providing reminder and follow-up phone calls; (d) utilising mail correspondence, including recognising children's birthdays and holidays; and (e) anticipating changes in employment and parent work schedules by offering flexible appointment times, including evenings and weekends. Process strategies may include: (a) establishing therapeutic rapport with the family; (b) praising parents for attendance; (c) encouraging a collaborative approach to therapy, such as empowering caregivers to use skills at home and in session to facilitate treatment; (d) preparing caregivers for the potential escalation of internalising and externalising behaviour problems during the exposure phase of treatment; (e) tracking symptom changes across treatment to help the child and caregiver visualise progress; (f) reviewing expectations with the child and caregiver; and (g) attending to overall family problems.

One of the strongest predictors of dropout is a therapeutic relationship problem (Ford 1978; Garcia and Weisz 2002). Arguably, trauma work, relative to traditional client-centred therapy, poses a higher risk for ruptures in the therapist's relationship with the child and caregiver due to the complicated nature of the work. This is especially true for special populations such as child welfare and juvenile justice. For example, children and caregivers involved with child protective services often maintain an adversarial relationship with the child welfare system and tend to object to interventions viewed as agency driven. Many children overseen by child protective services are fearful that something they say will further implicate their caregivers, prolong their placement in foster care or prompt removal if they are still residing in the home. Young people involved in juvenile justice services, where trauma-related problems are more prevalent than the general population, also face increased risk of dropout. Some lead transient lifestyles, moving from home to home, with little to no parental supervision. Incarceration, placement in residential treatment, social disaffiliation (e.g., runaway) and lack of parental guidance often result in low rates of admission and engagement (Grasso, Webb, Cohen and Berman 2012).

Start talking about the risk of dropout and missed appointments early on. Brainstorm possible barriers with the family. If a barrier emerges at some point during therapy, address it head on. Show the family how important it is to you by taking time to problem solve and offer support and assistance.

Handouts and Worksheets

Title

Worksheet 'Simple Symptom Checker'

Worksheet 'Simple Symptom Tracker'

Handout 'What Kinds of Things Can Be Traumatic?'

Handout 'Sexual Abuse'

Handout 'What is Traumatic Grief?'

Worksheet 'Sticky Notes on the Brain'

Worksheet 'Distress Scale'

Worksheet 'Mock Narrative of Witnessing Physical Assault and Loss'

Worksheet 'Mock Narrative of Domestic Violence'

Worksheet 'Mock Narrative of a Serious Car Accident'

Worksheet 'Mock Narrative of Child Sexual Abuse'

Worksheet 'Mock Narrative of Group Sexual Assault'

Worksheet 'Mock Narrative of a Natural Disaster'

Worksheet 'Mock Narrative of a School Shooting'

Worksheet 'Fear Hierarchy'

Worksheet 'Baseline Caregiver Interview'

Handout 'What Can Get in the Way of a Caregiver's Ability to Support the Traumatised Child?'

Handout 'Why Caregiver Involvement is Critical to Child Trauma Treatment'

Handout 'A Caregiver's Introduction to Child Traumatic Stress'

Handout 'How Trauma Treatment Works: For Caregivers'

Handout 'How to Talk to Your Children about Trauma'

Worksheet 'What is the Function of This Behaviour?'

Handout 'How to Recognise and Reinforce Improvement'

Handout 'When to Actively Ignore and When to Act'

Worksheet 'The Score Keeper'

WORKSHEET
Simple Symptom Checker

Instructions

Check off the problems on this page that you think affect any of the following:

- Schoolwork
- Relationships with friends
- Relationships with family
- Ability to finish projects

- Ability to have fun
- Ability to get along with people
- Day-to-day functioning
- Ability to take care of yourself

Problems

Having thoughts and reminders of the trauma stuck in my head ☐

Having dreams or nightmares ☐

Feeling almost like the trauma was happening again ☐

Getting really upset or physically ill when something reminds me of the trauma ☐

My body reacting in a bad way to reminders of the trauma ☐

Avoiding anything that has to do with the trauma ☐

Trying not to think about the trauma ☐

Feeling really bad about myself, other people or the world ☐

Blaming myself for what happened ☐

Feeling very sad, angry, fearful or ashamed ☐

Not really feeling interested in doing things any more ☐

Having a hard time enjoying myself or just feeling happy ☐

Being irritable ☐

Doing things that I know might get me or someone else hurt or in trouble ☐

Feeling like I am on high alert ☐

Feeling really jumpy ☐

Having a hard time concentrating on things ☐

Not getting a good sleep ☐

TOTAL NUMBER OF PROBLEMS EXPERIENCED = _____ OUT OF 18

Simple Symptom Tracker

Name: _____ Start Date: _____ / _____ / _____

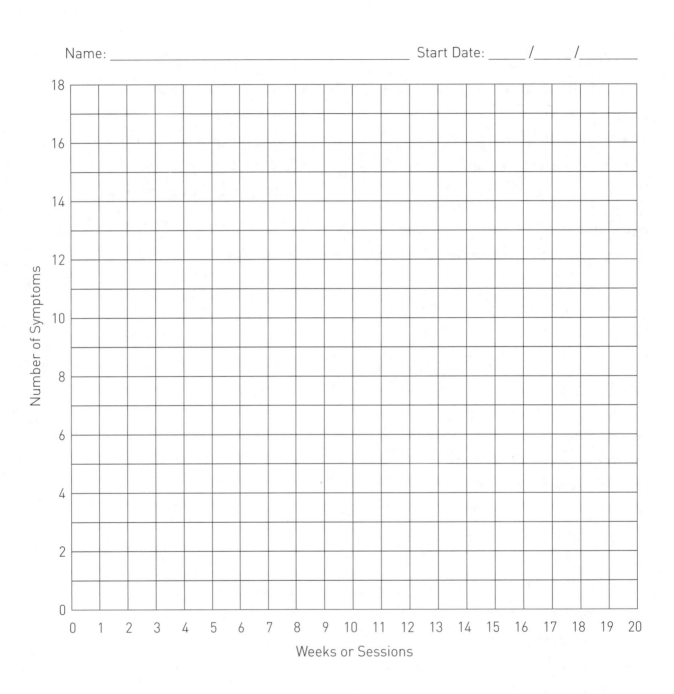

HANDOUT

What Kinds of Things Can Be Traumatic?

There are many different kinds of experiences that can be traumatic. These experiences include:

- someone dying

- you or someone else coming close to dying

- you or someone else being seriously hurt or injured

- you or someone else coming close to being seriously hurt or injured

- you or someone else being sexually assaulted

- you or someone else coming close to being sexually assaulted.

These things can be traumatic whether you experience the thing yourself, see it happening to someone else or hear about it happening to a close relative or close friend.

How common is it?

Experiencing something that could be traumatic is very common. In fact, almost all adults and most teenagers have experienced something that could be traumatic.

Does it happen more than once?

Many children have had more than one of these things happen to them over their lifetimes. On average, children who have experienced possible trauma have experienced two to three types of trauma. One might upset them more than the other, or they both might be equally upsetting.

Are there children who experience this many times?

Some children experience things that are possibly traumatic on an ongoing basis. These children may be abused or maltreated at home or grow up in very dangerous neighbourhoods.

Can you name some different kinds of possible trauma?

- Being in a *serious accident* such as a car or bike accident or one that causes death or serious injury.

- Being in a *very bad storm or natural disaster* such as a serious flood, tornado or earthquake that causes death or serious injury.

- Being *shot or shot at*, *beat up or badly hurt* in the neighbourhood or community.

- Seeing *family members fight* to the point where someone dies or could have died or someone is badly hurt.

- Being *bullied* to the point where someone gets hurt.

- Hearing that a *close relative or friend has died* or has been in a *serious accident* where he or she was badly hurt.

- Having a *very serious medical procedure* at a hospital.

- Being *hit, punched, kicked or badly hurt by a caregiver* or older adult in the home.
- Being in a place where there was *an actual war* going on.
- Being forced to *touch someone else's sexual body parts* or do *something sexual* with someone.
- Being *raped* or forced to have sex.

What makes these things traumatic?

These things are extreme stressors that put our brains and bodies into *survival mode*. In survival mode, the body goes through quick changes that prepare it to do what it has to do to survive. This might include running very fast, climbing, fighting back or doing something physically challenging. When this happens, the body shuts down certain functions in order to direct as much energy as possible to surviving. Even *thinking* gets turned down as there often isn't a lot of time to think. The body has to *react*. Because these things can be so intense, they become strong memories that are remembered easily. Some people have a hard time going from survival mode back to *everyday* mode. This means that their brain and body are acting as though there is still extreme danger. Being unable to switch out of survival mode can make it very hard to do things that don't have much to do with survival, such as pay attention at school, make new friends, solve problems and get along with other people.

Does everyone have problems after trauma?

People respond to things differently. Not everyone has a hard time switching from survival mode to everyday mode. Some children do not seem to have any problems after something traumatic. On the other hand, some children do have a hard time and need some help from experts. We don't really know why some children have problems after trauma and some don't. In part, it may have to do with differences in their genes. It also may have something to do with other life experiences they had. What is important, though, is that children who do have problems after a trauma can get better with the right help.

Sexual Abuse

What is sexual abuse?

Sexual abuse is when an adult or someone much older than you forces or influences you to have some type of sexual contact with them. Sexual contact can mean all kinds of things. It could mean kissing on the mouth or other areas of the body. It could mean the adult touching your private sexual body parts or having you touch his or her sexual body parts. It could mean the adult putting his or her mouth on your sexual body parts or having you put your mouth on his or her sexual body parts. It could mean the adult putting something in your private sexual body parts, including the vagina if you are a girl or the buttocks if you are a girl or boy.

How common is sexual abuse?

Sexual abuse happens to girls and boys of different races and from different areas. About one in every four girls and one in every six boys are sexually abused.

Who sexually abuses children and adolescents?

The abuser could be a man or a woman. Abusers are often someone you know and trust and can be a family member or someone close to you or your family. Children who are sexually abused can be young, such as between birth and five years old, or older, such as a teenager.

Why do abusers sexually abuse children and adolescents?

Abusers are more sexually attracted to young people and are people who give in to this attraction by forcing or influencing you to do something sexual with them. They make poor choices and are not good at controlling their behaviour. Sexual abuse is never the child or teen's fault.

How does sexual abuse affect the way children and adolescents behave?

Children have different reactions to sexual abuse. For some, sexual abuse can affect how they behave and feel. For example, some children have nightmares, have accidents in their bed at night, want to be alone most of the time, have problems at school or act-out. Other children may talk about sex a lot or show a lot of sexual behaviour. Sexual abuse can make children feel ashamed or bad about themselves, different from other children, very sad and very angry.

How do children and teens feel when they have been sexually abused?

Children can have all kinds of different feelings after sexual abuse happens. The sexual touching may actually feel good to some children, even though they don't like that it is happening. Some children like the person who did it because of the relationship they had. Other children are very angry towards the person who did it. Other children are very scared or feel guilty about what happened. Some children feel upset for a long time after the abuse has ended, but they often feel better after getting help.

Why don't some children tell about the abuse right away?

Sometimes the abuser tells the child or teen to keep the abuse a secret. The abuser might also use tricks to keep the child or teen from telling. The abuser may say that it is your fault or that you or your family will get hurt if you tell. Sometimes children keep it a secret because they feel ashamed, embarrassed or scared. Sometimes children need a little time to gain the courage to tell.

Can people tell that a child or teen has been sexually abused?

No. You cannot tell just by looking at a child or teen that he or she has been sexually abused. Sometimes you can see that something is bothering the child or teen but you do not know what that is.

HANDOUT
What is Traumatic Grief?

Is it normal to be upset after someone you love dies?

It is normal for children to *grieve* or feel very upset or deeply sorry after someone they love dies. Grieving children often feel very sad and may have trouble sleeping, feel less hungry and eat less, lose interest in spending time with family and friends, feel irritable and withdrawn, have trouble concentrating, and may think a lot about death. For some children it is normal to feel sick or have physical complaints or to go back to doing something that they have outgrown, such as bedwetting or wanting to stay very close to caregivers.

What kinds of things are not normal?

Some children develop something that we call *traumatic grief*. This is different from the normal grieving process. Children with traumatic grief often have the following problems related to the death:

- Being so upset that they cannot do normal everyday things, even three months after the death.
- Feeling horrified or terrified when they think of the death.
- Having ongoing nightmares and sleep problems even months after the death.
- Feeling guilty about the death and blaming themselves for it.
- Complaining of physical problems such as headaches or stomach aches.
- Having ongoing and bothersome thoughts or reminders about the way the person died.
- Starting to perform very badly in school.
- Remaining very irritable and angry even months after the death.
- Not *accepting* that the death actually happened.
- Withdrawing from friends and family and losing interest in doing social things even months after the death.

Sticky Notes on the Brain

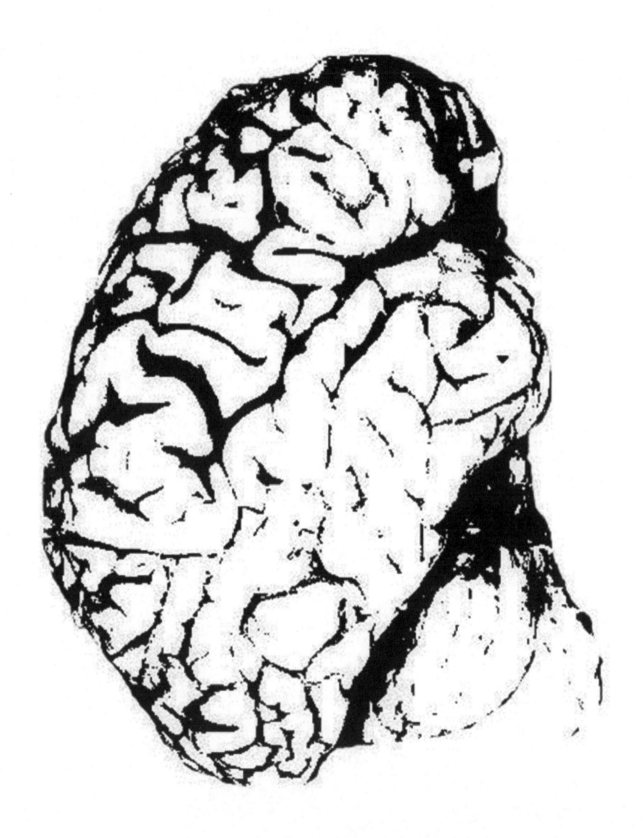

Distress Scale

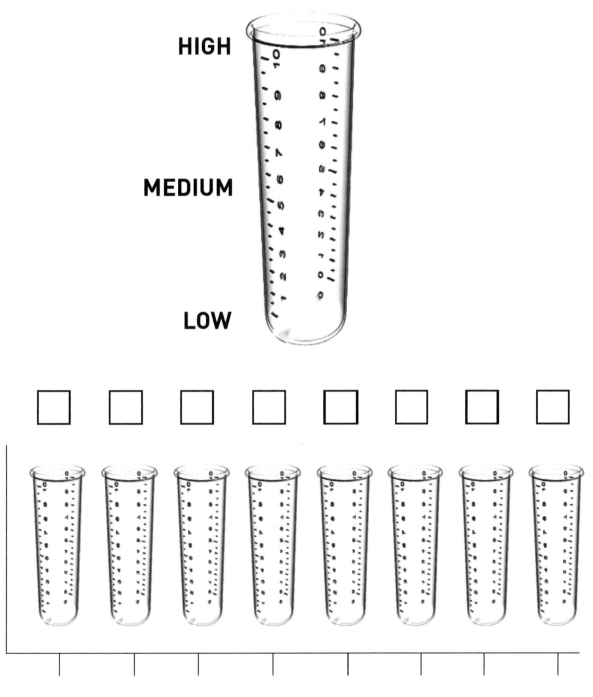

✓

Mock Narrative of Witnessing Physical Assault and Loss

Carla is an adolescent girl who witnessed her brother being physically assaulted by a group of other boys in her neighbourhood. Her brother suffered fatal injuries and was pronounced dead at the hospital. Carla opted to write her narrative in the form of a poem.

Procedures

Provide a brief introduction to Carla and her trauma narrative.

> *The trauma narrative I am going to show you was created by a girl around your age, named Carla. Carla was walking down the street in her neighbourhood when she saw a group of boys across the street beating up another boy. She didn't know it until later, but the boy they were beating up was her younger brother. She had witnessed terrible violence and experienced a significant loss. She decided to make her trauma narrative in the form of a poem. Let's take a look. [Read the poem to the child.] What do you think of this? [Let child respond.]*

Ask the child to find the spot where Carla describes her emotion.

> *Carla did a really great job. Can you pick out spots in the poem where Carla talks about how she was feeling during the trauma?*

Point out where Carla reveals her thought content.

> *Excellent. Now, can you find spots where Carla identifies what thoughts she was having at the time?*

Reflect on Carla's situation.

> *I want to tell you that Carla had a hard time talking about her brother's death. She did a lot of crying, and that is normal. When she wrote this poem I saw a lot of strength in her. She was able to face the trauma and the loss – and I think that made her feel confident that she could think about and talk about what happened on her own terms, without it getting stuck in her mind when she did not want it to.*

Ask the child whether he can relate to Carla's experience.

> *After looking at this, I am wondering whether there are any similarities between your experience and Carla's experience. What are your thoughts on that?*

If the child connects with his own experience, use more probing to transition the processing to the child's trauma experience.

Explore whether the child is open to incorporating interests or talents in creating his own trauma narrative.

FLOWERS ON MY MIND

they brought flowers to bury him
there were no flowers on the street that day
only scary looking boys with violence
on their faces
they were too far for me to see my brother
but close enough to feel the horror
one, two, three, four five six of them
taking the life away from
one
when I learned it was him
there was nothing I could do
to save him, though what
could I have really done
but love him
one
flower on his casket
stood up tallest
and that was my brother
never letting down
but I wish he did on that day
I wish he ducked way down
far away from the nonsense
that seems to walk the
streets where my family
lives, or tries to
when will it end?
flowers are prettier when
one
can look at them

Mock Narrative of Domestic Violence

Rafael is an 11-year-old boy who witnessed severe domestic violence between his mother and his stepfather. The worst incident and the focus of his narrative was when his stepfather beat her to the ground, threw a bottle at her and kicked her. She required medical care. Rafael attempted to intervene by posturing at his stepfather. In response, his stepfather threw him against the wall. He then went for help from the neighbours in the next apartment.

Procedures

Provide a brief introduction to Rafael and his trauma narrative.

The trauma narrative I am going to show you was created by a boy around your age, named Rafael. His narrative has to do with his being exposed to ongoing violence between his mother and his stepfather. He chose to focus on one particular incident when his stepfather hurt his mother and sent her to the hospital. Because Rafael was a creative guy and also liked to use computers, he chose to use an online programme that allows you to create your own comic book style strip. [www.bitstrips.com] Let's take a look.

Ask the child to find the spot where Rafael describes his emotion.

Rafael did a really great job. Let's read through the strip and keep an eye out for where Rafael identifies and states how he was feeling during the violence.

Point out where Rafael reveals his thought content.

Excellent. Now, can you find the spots where Rafael identifies what thoughts he was having at the time?

Reflect on Rafael's situation.

I want to tell you that Rafael had initially refused to talk about the domestic violence. It took him a while, but once he decided to face the trauma, he did an amazing job. He also found it easier to make the narrative when he was able to use his talent for drawing. He said it kept him focused.

Ask the child whether she can relate to Rafael's experience.

After looking at this, I am wondering whether there are any similarities between your experience and Rafael's experience. What are your thoughts on that?

If the child connects with her own experience, use more probing to transition the processing to the child's trauma experience.

Explore whether the child is open to incorporating interests or talents in creating her own trauma narrative.

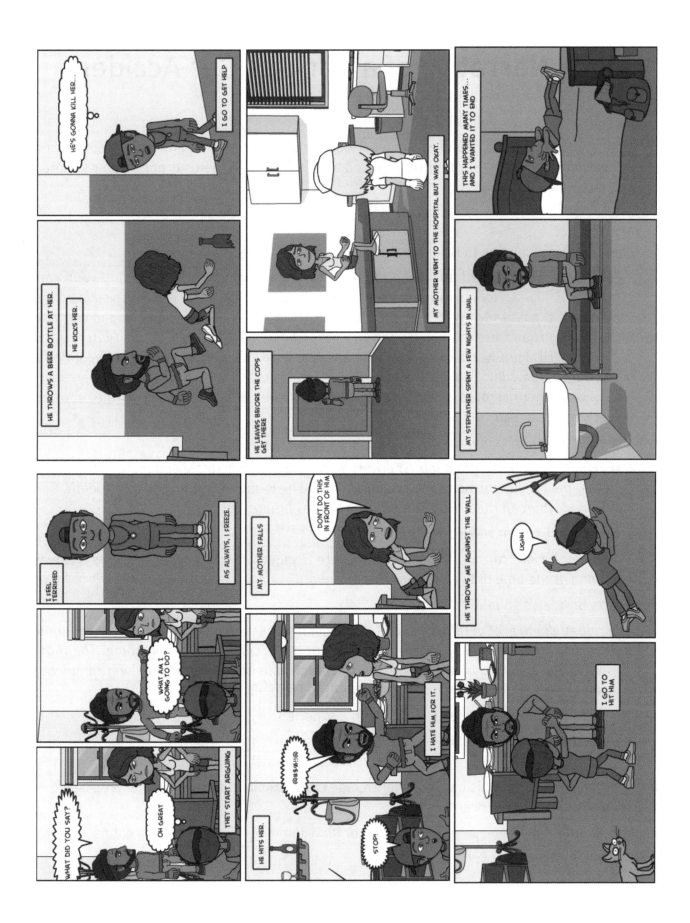

✓

Mock Narrative of a Serious Car Accident

Bridgett is a 12-year-old girl who was in a serious car accident involving her grandmother and another vehicle. A child in the other vehicle died on the scene. Bridgett's grandmother suffered critical injuries but survived.

Procedures

Provide a brief introduction to Bridgett and her trauma narrative.

> *The trauma narrative I am going to show you was created by a girl around your age, named Bridgett. Her narrative is about a serious car accident she was involved in where she was a passenger with her grandmother. They collided with another car carrying a young girl and her mother. The young girl, who was five years old, died later at the hospital. Bridgett was a bright girl who liked to write and was interested in becoming a journalist someday. She decided to use her journalism interest to write her narrative. She wrote her narrative as though it was a newspaper article and she was the reporter. Let's give it a read.*

Ask the child to find the spot where Bridgett describes her emotion.

> *Bridgett did a really great job. She worked hard on her narrative and included how she felt at the time of the accident, and later when she found out about the girl's death. Can you find where in the article she talks about her emotions?*

Point out where Bridgett reveals her thought content.

> *Excellent. Now, can you find the spots where Bridgett identifies what thoughts she was having at the time of the accident and afterward?*

Reflect on Bridgett's situation.

> *Bridgett spent a lot of time writing this article. It went through a lot of different versions. It wasn't completely easy for her to talk about the accident in the beginning. The more she wrote about it, however, the more comfortable she became thinking about her memory of the accident. This is what I want to happen for you.*

Ask the child whether he can relate to Bridgett's experience.

> *After looking at this, I am wondering whether there are any similarities between your experience and Bridgett's experience. What are your thoughts on that?*

If the child connects with his own experience, use more probing to transition the processing to the child's trauma experience.

Explore whether the child is open to incorporating interests or talents in creating his own trauma narrative.

HORRIFIC CAR ACCIDENT KILLS YOUNG GIRL

Also in the crash were a ten-year-old girl and her grandmother. The child suffered minor injuries.

Monday 13 June. Girl and her mother were on their way to the playground

On Monday, a ten-year-old girl and her grandmother were involved in a fatal crash with a five-year-old girl and her mother. The five-year-old girl suffered fatal injuries. Ten-year-old Bridgett described the crash as sudden and terrifying. She was riding in the back seat when she was suddenly pulled forward with a lot of force. She hit her head on the seat in front of her. Her body hurt immediately. She felt sudden terror and immediately thought about the safety of her grandmother who was driving the car. When she looked up towards the driver, all she could see was blood everywhere. She still remembers the look of it. According to the girl it seemed like forever before firemen cut

her seatbelt and pulled her out of the car. She felt stunned. She saw her grandmother being taken from the car in a stretcher. She also saw someone in the other car being taken away in a stretcher. She later learned that the young five-year-old girl in the other car had died at the hospital. When she learned that the other girl died, she felt so sad. She also felt guilty even though the crash was considered an accident caused by the other driver. Bridgett was relieved when she got to see her grandmother later. Her grandmother looked beat up but was going to be okay. She thought about the young girl a lot. She remembered when she was that age and could not imagine losing her life like this. She also felt very sad for the mother who lost her daughter. This was a tragic day for both families.

WORKSHEET
Mock Narrative of Child Sexual Abuse

Kyle is a 14-year-old boy with a history of sexual abuse by a male friend of the family who had babysat for him between the ages of seven and eight. Kyle revealed the abuse only about a year ago. Kyle also has experienced other adversity including family drug and alcohol problems and having unstable housing.

Procedures

Provide a brief introduction to Kyle and his trauma narrative.

> *The trauma narrative I am going to show you was created by a boy around your age, named Kyle. Kyle's narrative has to do with his being sexually abused by a male friend of the family when he was between the ages of seven and eight. Kyle kept this to himself for many years and just told about it when he was 13. Even though the sexual abuse had stopped, it had been causing him problems at home and at school. Kyle was a pretty creative child. He was studying symbols in school and was very interested in tribal markings and stuff. His mother, who had passed away when he was about ten, was from South America, and so Kyle was particularly interested in symbols from that area, where tribes often used symbols on their face and on their clothing for ceremonies. He decided it would be neat to use symbols in his trauma narrative to tell his story. Let's take a look.*

> *So, Kyle put a picture of himself on the computer and used a drawing software programme to put markings on his face. He then explained what each of the symbols represented and used them to tell his narrative.*

Ask the child to find the spot where Kyle describes his emotion.

> *Kyle did a really great job. Let's read through the strip and keep an eye out for where Kyle identifies and states how he was feeling during the violence.*

Point out where Kyle reveals his thought content.

> *Excellent. Now, can you find the spots where Kyle identifies what thoughts he was having at the time?*

Reflect on Kyle's situation.

> *I want to tell you that it took Kyle a long time to talk about the sexual abuse. Even in therapy, Kyle initially could not get himself to talk about it. Once he decided to face the abuse, he did an amazing job. He also found it easier to make the narrative when he was able to incorporate his interest in symbols and South America. He said it kept him focused.*

Ask the child whether she can relate to Kyle's experience.

> *After looking at this, I am wondering whether there are any similarities between your experience and Kyle's experience. What are your thoughts on that?*

If the child connects with her own experience, use more probing to transition the processing to the child's trauma experience.

Explore whether the child is open to incorporating interests or talents in creating her own trauma narrative.

This symbolises the things I had to overcome to get where I am now. The two straight lines represent a road and the jagged lines represent things that get in the way. For me this was the sexual abuse that happened to me. This symbol is from the culture of native Ecuador tribes.

This is a symbol of a crescent moon. It reminds me of my mother because she would always say that it was God smiling down on me. Since my mother died now when I see it I kind of think of it as my mother smiling down on me. I feel like she helped me get through this in my life.

These represent my brother and sisters who I care about a lot and who help me in a lot of ways.

This is a symbol of a bear and is supposed to stand for courage and bravery. I feel like I had to be strong to look back at the times I was abused. It was always something I tried to forget. When I did work on it I realised that there isn't anything to fear now. I didn't feel brave at the time of the abuse because I felt like I was doing something wrong and that I should have been able to stop him from abusing me.

These stand for the 12 times that I can remember being sexually abused. Some times were worse than others. I felt like I became frozen, like I couldn't move. I did not know how to stop it because I felt paralysed.

This is a symbol of a serpent and it represents the person who had sexually abused me. He had tricked me into giving him my trust and then abused me. I felt betrayed. I also felt like I couldn't trust people any more. I kept thinking that I did something wrong. I also thought that there was something wrong with me because I was sexually abused.

Mock Narrative of Group Sexual Assault

Jenna is a 16-year-old teenager who was raped by a group of older boys in a park near the school. The assault happened less than a year ago.

Procedures

Provide a brief introduction to Jenna and her trauma narrative.

> *The trauma narrative I am going to share with you was created by a girl around your age, named Jenna. Jenna was walking home from school through a park when she was approached by a group of boys who raped her. Jenna chose to type out her trauma narrative. She made a number of changes since the first version of it. The one you are going to read is something like the sixth version. Let's give it a read.*

Ask the child to find the spot where Jenna describes her emotion.

> *Jenna did an amazing job. Can you pick out spots in the narrative where she talks about how she was feeling during the trauma?*

Point out where Jenna reveals her thought content.

> *Excellent. Now, can you find spots where Jenna identifies what thoughts she was having at the time?*

Reflect on Jenna's situation.

> *Jenna did some very challenging work. She did not want to talk about the sexual assault, but when she started writing about it, it became easier for her. She said that the more she wrote the more in control of herself she felt. And that is one of the points – to take back control of what was taken from you.*

Ask the child whether he can relate to Jenna's experience.

> *After looking at this, I am wondering whether there are any similarities between your experience and Jenna's experience. What are your thoughts on that?*

If the child connects with his own experience, use more probing to transition the processing to the child's trauma experience.

Explore whether the child is open to incorporating interests or talents in creating his own trauma narrative.

WALKING THROUGH THE PARK

I am already having a bad day because I failed a test at school. I stayed at school late in order to get some extra credit on it. When I leave the sun is starting to get lower. It is pretty at this time of day. It made me feel a little better. I decide to use a shortcut to get back home by cutting through a park. It is a park I go to a lot just to think about things. I feel safe. When I get further into the park I see a group of boys walking and laughing. I see that they notice me. One of them gestures to me. I don't make too much of it but I do feel a little nervous. Then I notice that they are starting to walk in my direction. I get a little bit more nervous. They are walking faster. When they get to me one of them says something to me. I don't even remember what he said. The next thing I know one of the boys hits me across my butt and another one comes in close to me. I know at this point that I'm in trouble. It is somewhat a blur after that. I am pushed to the ground and I feel them all around me. Touching me. I feel hands up my shirt and touching my breasts. Someone is unbuttoning my pants and pulling them down to my knees. I am yelling for them to stop. I can hear one of them saying to get them off quick, meaning my pants. I feel hands going into my underwear and touching my vagina. They are putting their fingers in my vagina. They get my pants off and I can make out one of the boys with his pants down. He is kneeling and he is holding on to his penis and putting it in my vagina. Other boys are holding down my legs and egging him on. He puts it in and I can feel pain shoot up my body. He is rough. I am too terrified to feel anything. Someone else pushes him aside and does the same thing. I am paralysed. Then I hear one of them say that they have to get out of here and they run off. I am laying on the ground. I am hurting. I am scared. I feel dirty. My clothes are half off and I'm just crying. Someone hears me and eventually help comes and I make my way to the hospital.

✓

Mock Narrative of a Natural Disaster

Jamie is a 12-year-old boy whose family lost their home due to a tornado. After the storm Jamie was the first to witness an elderly neighbour who had been dismembered and killed by the impact of a vehicle wrapped around a tree in the yard.

Procedures

Provide a brief introduction to Jamie and his trauma narrative.

The trauma narrative I am going to share with you is from a boy about your age, named Jamie. He was having traumatic stress due to being in a tornado with his family and seeing an older neighbour who had been killed by the tornado. He chose to write his narrative. Jamie wrote a number of versions of the narrative and the one I am going to show you is about the sixth version. Every time he would write a new version he would try to add more detail or add information about how he was feeling or what he was thinking. Let's give it a read.

Ask the child to find the spot where Jamie describes his emotion.

Jamie did a really great job. After listening to his narrative, can you find the spots where he talks about how he was feeling?

Point out where Jamie reveals his thought content.

Excellent. Now, can you find the spots where Jamie identifies what thoughts he was having at the time?

Reflect on Jamie's situation.

Jamie did a lot of hard work. It was not always easy for him to think about his trauma memory, especially when he comes across his neighbour. After confronting the trauma memory, however, it becomes easier for Jamie to think about and talk about the trauma. In the end he was proud of having done the narrative.

Ask the child whether she can relate to Jamie's experience.

After looking at this, I am wondering whether there are any similarities between your experience and Jamie's experience. What are your thoughts on that?

If the child connects with her own experience, use more probing to transition the processing to the child's trauma experience.

Explore whether the child is open to incorporating interests or talents in creating her own trauma narrative.

WORKSHEET
Mock Narrative of a School Shooting

Natalia is an eight-year-old girl who was a student at school where a gunman unexpectedly walked in and killed several students and teachers before taking his own life. Natalia's class was spared but she heard the gunshots and the screams happening in the classroom next door.

Procedures

Provide a brief introduction to Natalia and her trauma narrative.

> *The trauma narrative I am going to share with you was created by a girl around your age, named Natalia. Natalia was in school when someone came in and shot and killed a number of students in the classroom next to hers. She heard the gunshots and what was happening. She talks about her experience that day in her trauma narrative. She chose to use pictures and words to create the narrative. Let's take a look at it.*

Ask the child to find the spot where Natalia describes her emotion.

> *Natalia did an amazing job. Can you pick out spots in the narrative where she talks about how she was feeling during the trauma?*

Point out where Natalia reveals her thought content.

> *Excellent. Now, can you find spots where Natalia identifies what thoughts she was having at the time?*

Reflect on Natalia's situation.

> *Natalia did some very challenging work. It was hard for her to talk about this experience at first, but the more she worked on the narrative, the easier it was for her. She began to think more and focus on some of the positive things that happened to her – like her father being there to support and comfort her afterwards.*

Ask the child whether he can relate to Natalia's experience.

> *After looking at this, I am wondering whether there are any similarities between your experience and Natalia's experience. What are your thoughts on that?*

If the child connects with his own experience, use more probing to transition the processing to the child's trauma experience.

Explore whether the child is open to incorporating interests or talents in creating his own trauma narrative.

✓

It was a normal day. I was in math Class. I was feeling bored.

We heard some strange noises. My teacher looked a little worried.

1

I heard police cars outside. I could not see them but it sounded like a lot.

I hoped they would get here fast.

4

Then my teacher looked very scared. I thought something was wrong. Other kids started talking and some got out of their seats. I stayed in my seat but then the teacher told us to get behind the desk with her.

2

When it was over they told us to close our eyes as we walked out.

People were crying. When I got out my dad ran over to me and hugged me. He was crying.

5

We heard loud bangs and people screaming I felt very scared.

I thought We were going to be hurt and that we were next.

3

A lot of people were crying. I was told that kids in a class next to me were killed by a man with a gun.

I wondered why someone would do that. It made my body feel sick.

6

Fear Hierarchy

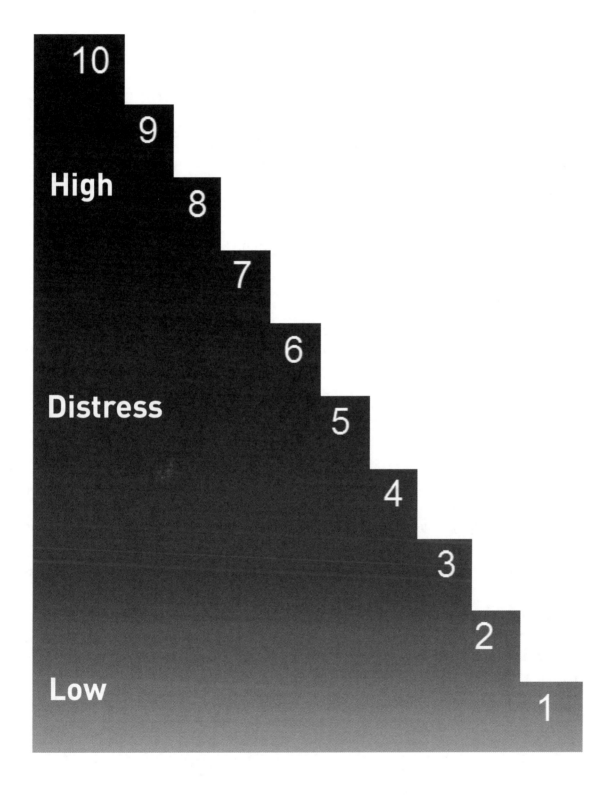

Baseline Caregiver Interview

Family relationships

1. How would you describe your relationship with your child? What are the strengths of your relationship? What do you wish was better about your relationship? Does your child talk to you about personal things?

2. Describe other relationships you and the child have in the home – other caregivers, children, relatives, etc. Any family violence? Frequent arguments?

3. What do you and your child do for fun?

4. How has the child's trauma affected his or her relationship with you and other members of the family?

5. How would you describe your approach to parenting? Discipline? Limit-setting? Do you feel effective as a parent? What could you do better as a parent?

Family stressors

1. Have there been any significant stressors (besides the trauma) in the family in the past several months? *Death of a relative, financial problems, medical procedures, death of a pet, etc.*

2. If yes, how have you and the family been coping with the stressor(s)? If no, how does your family typically cope with significant stressors?

3. Has it had an impact on family relationships? Or, how does stress typically affect your family relationships?

Caregiver history

1. What was it like for you growing up as a child? What were relationships like in your family? Adversity? Resilience?

2. How do you think your relationship with your caregiver(s) has influenced your approach to parenting?

3. As a child, have you ever experienced something that was potentially traumatic or extremely stressful? *Child physical or sexual abuse, assault, witnessed family violence, serious accident, death of a loved one, etc.* If yes, did this cause any problems for you?

4. How about as an adult; have you ever experienced something that was potentially traumatic or extremely stressful? *Physical or sexual assault, intimate partner violence, death of a loved one, community violence, etc.* If yes, did this cause any problems for you?

5. [If past trauma] How has your experiencing past trauma or violence influenced the way you have responded to your own child's trauma? Has your child's trauma made you think more about your past trauma? Did symptoms worsen? Did your past trauma make it hard to think about or deal with your child's trauma exposure?

6. [If past trauma] Have you ever talked about your past trauma with your child? If so, what was his or her response?

7. Have you ever had any mental health problems in the past or currently? *Depression, anxiety, addiction, etc.* Have you received treatment for it? Will it get in the way of your involvement in your son or daughter's therapy?

8. Have you ever considered receiving your own therapy either because of an existing mental health problem or because of your child's trauma?

Child's trauma

1. How did you learn about your child's [trauma] and what was your reaction?

2. How did you respond to your child once you found out about the trauma?

3. Does your child talk to you about the trauma?

4. What bothers you most about what happened?

5. How do you think your child's trauma will influence his or her future?

Treatment expectations

1. How did you find out about this programme?

2. What do you hope this programme will do for your child?

3. How will you know that this programme is working for your child?

4. Do you know anything about how the treatment approach we use? *Exposure-based therapy, cognitive behavioural therapy, etc.*

Potential barriers

1. What do you think might get in the way of the child's treatment?

2. What happens if your child decides he or she does not want to come to treatment?

3. Will you be willing to commit to getting your child to treatment each week?

4. Is there anything else that would cause you to terminate treatment before your child has completed the programme?

Ask additional questions as deemed appropriate.

What Can Get in the Way of a Caregiver's Ability to Support the Traumatised Child?

Parenting the traumatised child is a challenging task that requires caregivers to take a look at their own wellbeing and to increase their personal resources. Parenting in the absence of trauma is difficult. Child trauma exposure adds another layer of difficulty to parenting. Trauma exposure can lead to child emotional and behavioural problems and can interrupt normal child development in ways that can be confusing and frustrating to caregivers. It is critical that caregivers are optimally supported and resourced to meet the challenges associated with child trauma. Too often, the effect of a child's trauma exposure on the caregiver and the caregiver's own needs are ignored. Ignoring these needs, however, fails fully to implement an effective intervention for the child.

What can get in the way of my ability to support my child?

- Untreated depression
- Untreated anxiety
- Alcohol or substance misuse
- Intimate partner violence
- Post-traumatic stress disorder
- Poor stress management
- Family conflict
- Complicated grief

Links between unaddressed caregiver problems and child functioning

- Depressed caregivers tend to show less positive and more negative interactions with their children including (a) less praise for accomplishment, (b) fewer happy facial expressions, (c) less affection, (d) more irritability, (e) greater focus on unwanted behaviour, and (f) less emotional availability.

- Depressed caregivers tend to feel less competent in their parenting and perceive their relationship with their child as less positive.

- Children with a depressed caregiver tend to show more depressed affect, disruptive behaviour problems and difficulty getting along with other people.

- Clinically anxious caregivers tend to (a) have difficulty paying attention to their child's needs, (b) withdraw from and avoid their child's trauma exposure and resultant symptoms and distress, and (c) become easily overwhelmed by their child's needs.

- Greater parental conflict following a child's trauma is associated with more severe symptoms of post-traumatic stress in children.
- Greater parental stress is associated with poorer outcomes in children exposed to trauma.
- Post-traumatic stress in caregivers is directly associated with children's post-traumatic stress.
- Trauma-exposed children with caregivers with untreated anxiety, depression or alcoholism have more severe post-traumatic stress than trauma-exposed children with relatively healthy caregivers.

What can caregivers do to optimise personal resources and their ability to support their child in therapy?

Ask yourself these questions:

- How has my child's trauma affected my ability to parent?
- Have I struggled with depression, anxiety or some other mental health problem in the past?
- Has it worsened since my child's trauma exposure?
- Has past trauma exposure interfered with my ability to accept and address my child's trauma?
- Have I been thinking more about my trauma exposure?
- Am I at the *end of my rope*?

If you answered 'yes' to any of these questions, it may be time to take steps towards helping yourself to recover. Standing by your child throughout the therapy process requires you to become emotionally involved and to draw on strengths and resources to help guide your child to recovery. Insufficient resources and emotional turmoil will hinder your ability to do that.

Where can I find help?

You can take steps towards getting help by talking to your primary care provider or contacting a mental health professional directly. Sometimes a primary care provider can adequately treat depression and anxiety; however, other times it may take a mental health professional to do the best job. There are a number of different types of mental health professionals including psychiatrists, who generally prescribe medication, psychiatric nurses, who can also prescribe medication, psychologists with PhDs and PsyDs, who generally provide assessment and psychotherapy, and clinical social workers and licensed professional counsellors, among others, who provide individual and family counselling and therapy.

✓

HANDOUT

Why Caregiver Involvement is Critical to Child Trauma Treatment

Treatment outcome

Traumatised children who have caregivers who actively participate in their treatment show greater reductions in post-traumatic stress, depression and disruptive behaviours following treatment than children whose caregivers are not engaged in treatment.

How can caregivers engage in their child's treatment and encourage positive outcomes?

The caregiver...

- is willing and able to engage in discussions with the child about the trauma and associated feelings and thoughts

- explores how the child's trauma has affected him or her and his or her relationship with the child

- makes connections between his or her past childhood and adult experiences, including potential trauma exposure, and what the child is going through

- models for the child healthy ways of coping with stress and trauma reminders

- encourages the child to apply principles learned in therapy to situations outside of therapy

- pulls together social support and partners in recovery

- becomes a strong advocate for the child

- motivates the child to engage in treatment

- frequently praises the child for his or her trauma work and for confronting fears

- participates in conjoint therapy sessions when encouraged to do so

- strives to make regular appointments

- monitors his or her child's progress over time.

A Caregiver's Introduction to Child Traumatic Stress

How is trauma defined?

An event has the potential to be traumatic if it involves exposure to death or threatened death, serious injury or illness, or sexual violence that has either been directly experienced, witnessed happening to someone else, or heard about happening to someone close to you. A majority of children 16 years or older have at some point in their lives been exposed to an event with the potential of being traumatic. Trauma occurs when such an event elicits powerful emotional and behavioural responses. These responses last longer than the duration of the threat or danger. In the presence of danger, the stress response is adaptive. It helps us to survive by putting our bodies into *emergency or survival mode*. For some children, coming out of survival mode and readjusting to everyday life is difficult – as if they become stuck. Other children spend a good portion of their childhood in *survival mode* because they are exposed to chronic adversity and stress. For these children, being in this mode has become the norm.

What are common symptoms of traumatic stress?

1. Having intrusive and distressing memories of the event.

2. Having frightening dreams or nightmares with content that is not necessarily related to the event.

3. Feeling or acting as if the event were happening again – which may result in a complete loss of awareness of present surroundings.

4. Disturbing and long-lasting psychological distress when exposed to reminders of the event.

5. Intense bodily reactions to reminders of the event.

6. Deliberate avoidance of trauma reminders, which may include memories, thoughts or feelings, as well as people, places, things and situations.

7. Having developed negative beliefs about self, others and the world after the event.

8. Being in a persistent negative emotional state since the event.

What can be done about it?

Decades of research have led to the development of several therapies to treat child traumatic stress. One of the most common and well-studied models is Trauma-Focused Cognitive Behavioural Therapy (TF-CBT). TF-CBT is a 12- to 16-session programme whereby the child learns a variety of coping and problem-solving skills and, with the help of a therapist, develops a written trauma narrative – a written account of the child's memory of the trauma. The purpose of the trauma narrative is to facilitate therapeutic exposure. Therapeutic exposure is a strategy in which repeated *exposure* to the child's trauma memory trains the child's body and brain not to be reactive to it any more. In other words, it teaches the child that the trauma memory is *just a memory* and does not pose any threat at the present. The trauma narrative also helps the child to better understand what happened, gain a sense of personal control over the situation, and add *new information* to the trauma memory that has healing or protective properties. This happens because memories are dynamic and can take on new information – like writing another chapter of a book. Helping your child to connect to a therapy that has been shown to be effective through research is the first step towards the child's recovery.

What can we do at home?

Children and adolescents will need your encouragement and support to express challenging emotions related to the trauma such as anger, fear, sadness, shame and worry. Convey the idea that these feelings and challenges are common in children with traumatic stress and that there are ways of improving these symptoms. You can also be a strong advocate for your child. Oftentimes traumatic stress will get in the way of the child's ability to perform well in school and to get along with other children. You can inform the school that this is a particularly difficult time for your child and assure them that your child is getting the help needed. Most important is for you to be a stable source of support to your child.

HANDOUT
How Trauma Treatment Works
For Caregivers

Is there evidence that treatment works?

Yes, decades of research have been conducted. The overall approach to treating traumatic stress, and all anxiety problems more generally, is therapeutic exposure. It has been used with children, adolescents and adults with a great deal of success. Although not all children respond to treatment, the greater majority do, and exposure-based therapy is our best approach thus far.

How does therapeutic exposure work?

Therapeutic exposure is when a person *habituates to* or becomes less reactive to something that is feared after repeat exposure to the feared stimuli. For example, imagine that you are terrified of flying in a plane. Now imagine slowly familiarising yourself with the plane by looking at pictures of planes, watching a video of people in a plane, seeing a plane close up, getting into a plane and sitting on the tarmac, and eventually going on a short plane ride. Each time you do something involving a plane, you feel nervous and uncomfortable, but after a while, your body starts to relax. We use the same approach when treating traumatic stress, only instead of using a plane, we are using the trauma memory. Because the trauma memory is not a concrete object that we can approach and touch, we must *activate* the trauma memory by writing about it or visualising it.

How does trauma memory processing work?

The goal of trauma memory processing is to help the child to organise the, often fragmented, trauma memory into a cohesive, and better-managed narrative. By reviewing the narrative and exploring the child's feelings and thoughts, during the trauma and at present, the child is gaining a better understanding of the trauma and how it has influenced his or her belief system, relationships and outlook on life. Essentially, the child is no longer *avoiding* the trauma memory, but has accepted it and has *added new information* into it that makes it less distressing.

How long does it take?

The length of therapy depends on the child; however, positive outcomes tend to be seen anytime between the fifth and fifteenth session. Attending therapy on a regular basis (i.e., weekly) without a long interval in between sessions will move the child along faster than if the child frequently misses appointments or goes long periods without seeing the therapist. In these cases, therapists often have to review old material, and are sometimes forced to start back at square one.

Is the child–therapist relationship important?

Yes, indeed. One of the most influential factors in therapy is the patient–therapist working relationship. This is too often overlooked. A child is unlikely to engage in therapeutic exposure and share personal details of physical or sexual abuse, the loss of a loved one or a horrific accident unless the child trusts the therapist and sees the therapist as someone who will listen to and understand what the child has to say. It is difficult to measure the child–therapist relationship, but it is a key factor in the therapy's success. There does not appear to be strong evidence to suggest that certain therapist characteristics (e.g., sex, race) are better matches for certain patients. It really depends on the patient. Caregivers can discuss how the child feels about the therapist outside of session and monitor the relationship. There may be ruptures in the relationship, and this is okay. In fact, ruptures can lead to positive change. The important thing is that the therapist is engaging the child and facilitating change.

How To Talk to Your Children About Trauma

What to do when your child brings up the trauma at the dinner table...

As children process the trauma memory in session and outside of session they are prone to *bringing up* the trauma in conversation at home. These are opportunities to facilitate healthy discussions about the trauma and extend the work that is being done in therapy. These opportunities may happen at unusual times: in the car on the way to school, before bedtime, around the dinner table, in a text message, etc. Perhaps the child makes a statement about how he or she feels about the trauma (e.g., 'I was always scared to speak my mind when he was around') or a matter-of-fact statement having to do with the trauma (e.g., 'That's where it occurred – right over there on that corner'). Perhaps the child asks a question having to do with you (e.g., 'How did you last so long with someone who beat you?'). What you can do is be ready to respond in a way that will help your child to better understand the trauma, as well as to feel closer to you. Below are some suggested guidelines for talking to your child about the trauma.

Guidelines for talking about the trauma

1. Explore your personal feelings about your child's trauma exposure. Anticipate your reactions and think about how they may affect your child. You might do this by sharing your feelings with other adults or professionals, or by writing in a journal.

2. Catch yourself when you attempt to avoid talking about the child's trauma. Work on reducing avoidance of trauma-related discussion and show your child that you are willing to talk openly about it.

3. Encourage trauma-related discussion gradually. For example, you might start with discussions that are more general (e.g., how someone *else* who experienced sexual abuse might feel), slowly moving towards discussion about the child's personal experience (e.g., how the child feels about being sexually abused).

4. Sometimes caregivers ask questions that unintentionally encourage children to feel as if they did something wrong. To avoid encouraging feelings of shame or self-blame, ask questions in ways that are supportive. For example, instead of saying, 'Why didn't you tell me sooner', you might say, 'What made you decide to tell when you did?'

5. Use open-ended questions. Questions that are phrased to elicit one-word responses often end with the one-word response. Therapists are trained to ask questions that necessitate more involved responses. For example, instead of saying, 'Do you feel like you have a better understanding of what happened that day?', you might say, 'You've done a lot of work in therapy. How do you think working with the therapist has given you a better understanding of what happened that day?'

6. Allow the child to set the pace of the conversation. Do not pressure the child to talk more than he or she wants to. This will discourage the child from talking in the future. When the child is finished, allow the conversation to end.

✓

What is the Function of This Behaviour?

STEP ONE	STEP TWO	STEP THREE	STEP FOUR	STEP FIVE
What is the behaviour?	What usually comes before the behaviour?	What usually happens because of the behaviour?	What is the possible function of the behaviour?	What can be done to alter this pattern?

HANDOUT

How to Recognise and Reinforce Improvement

Caregivers often underestimate the influence that their attention can have on their children's behaviours. Disruptive behaviour naturally draws a lot of caregiver attention. Sometimes caregivers are so used to attending to disruptive behaviours that they stop noticing the positive behaviours. This is not surprising. Disruptive behaviour often demands attention, whereas positive behaviour can be subtle. The thing is, positive reinforcement of behaviour is more powerful than punishment. This means that reinforcing positive behaviour will lead to greater behaviour change. So it is important to reward *improved* behaviour. Improvement might mean that the unwanted behaviour is occurring less often. It is not easy to recognise these subtle improvements in the midst of unwanted behaviour. However, as caregivers wanting to encourage positive behaviour change, we need to get into the habit of identifying improvement and providing praise for it.

General guidelines on positive reinforcement

1. Praise the behaviour as soon as you observe it.

2. Do this on a consistent basis so that your child starts to predict when his or her positive behaviour will be rewarded with your attention.

3. Be specific about what you are praising.

4. Be careful not to add on a negative twist to the praise (e.g., 'You handled that very well... but, you should be doing that more often').

5. Smile and express that you are happy with his or her behaviour.

6. Avoid praising for the sake of praising – make sure it is tied to a behaviour.

7. Recognise improved but imperfect behaviour. Notice when your child has made a subtle step towards ultimately reaching a particular behavioural goal.

8. What are some specific behaviours or signs of improvements that you might praise your child for the next time you notice them?

When to Actively Ignore and When to Act

Your attention, positive or negative, is rewarding to your child

It does not seem rational to ignore your child's *bad* behaviour, but sometimes that is the very thing that you should do. Think about it. When you are paying attention to your child's behaviour, good or bad, you are providing your child with your undivided attention. This is rewarding to your child. The very act of trying to stop the behaviour may be causing more of it to happen!

If the behaviour is unwanted, but not serious, ignoring it will remove the reward (your undivided attention) and might reduce the chances that your child will do it again next time.

Actively ignoring unwanted but less serious behaviour and praising positive behaviour and signs of improvement are the best strategies to promote behaviour change.

What are some mildly unwanted behaviours from your child or teen that you might ignore?

When behaviour is more serious or disruptive, be firm and directive, but try not to raise your voice. Raising your voice only increases the chances that you will get involved in a power struggle or screaming match with your child. Keeping the tone of your voice steady or lowering your voice may actually force your child to have to slow down in order to hear what you are saying. It is common for people to match the tone of their voice with the person they are talking to without even realising it. This does not stop you from being firm and directive, however. You should be firm and directive, making clear the consequence that your child will face should he or she choose to continue the behaviour. Consequences are successful when they are (a) enforceable, (b) important to your child, (c) consistent, (d) predictable, and (e) short in duration. Also, leave room to increase the magnitude of the consequence, otherwise you will no longer have any leverage over the behaviour should it continue.

WORKSHEET

The Score Keeper

Template

References

Aderka, I. M., Appelbaum-Namdar, E., Shafran, N. and Gilboa-Schechtman, E. (2011) 'Sudden gains in prolonged exposure for children and adolescents with posttraumatic stress disorder.' *Journal of Consulting and Clinical Psychology* *79*(4), 441–446.

Ahrens, J. and Rexford, L. (2002) 'Cognitive processing therapy for incarcerated adolescents with PTSD.' *Journal of Aggression, Maltreatment & Trauma* *6*(1), 201–216.

Babson, K. A., Badour, C. L., Feldner, M. T. and Bunaciu, L. (2012) 'The relationship of sleep quality and PTSD to anxious reactivity from idiographic traumatic event script-driven imagery.' *Journal of Traumatic Stress* *25* 5, 503–510.

Bigfoot, D. S. and Schmidt, S. R. (2010) 'Honoring children, mending the circle: cultural adaptation of trauma-focused cognitive-behavioral therapy for American Indian and Alaska native children.' *Journal of Clinical Psychology* *66*(8), 847–856.

Bonanno, G. A. (2008) 'Loss, trauma, and human resilience: Have we underestimated the human capacity to thrive after extremely aversive events?' *Psychological Trauma: Theory, Research, Practice, and Policy* *S*(1), 101–113.

Bonanno, G. A., Westphal, M. and Mancini, A. D. (2011) 'Resilience to loss and potential trauma.' *Annual Review of Clinical Psychology* *7*, 511–535.

Brewin, C. R. and Holmes, E. A. (2003) 'Psychological theories of posttraumatic stress disorder.' *Clinical Psychology Review. Special Issue: Post Traumatic Stress Disorder* *23*(3), 339–376.

Brewin, C. R., Andrews, B. and Valentine, J. D. (2000) 'Meta-analysis of risk factors for posttraumatic stress disorder in trauma-exposed adults.' *Journal of Consulting & Clinical Psychology* *68*(5), 748–766.

Bryant, R. A., Moulds, M. L., Mastrodomenico, J., Hopwood, S., Felmingham, K. L. and Nixon, R. D. V. (2007) 'Who drops out of treatment for post-traumatic stress disorder?' *Clinical Psychologist* *11*(1), 13–15.

Charuvastra, A. and Cloitre, M. (2008) 'Social bonds and posttraumatic stress disorder.' *Annual Review of Psychology* *59*, 301–328.

Cloitre, M., Stovall-McClough, K. C., Nooner, K., Zorbas, P. *et al.* (2010) 'Treatment for PTSD related to childhood abuse: A randomized controlled trial.' *The American Journal of Psychiatry* *167*(8), 915–924.

Cohen, J. A., Berliner, L. and Mannarino, A. (2010) 'Trauma focused CBT for children with co-occurring trauma and behavior problems.' *Child Abuse & Neglect* *34*(4), 215–224.

Cohen, J. A., Mannarino, A. P. and Deblinger, E. (2006) *Treating Trauma and Traumatic Grief in Children and Adolescents.* New York, NY: Guilford Press.

Cohen, J. A., Mannarino, A. P. and Knudsen, K. (2005) 'Treating sexually abused children: 1 year follow-up of a randomized controlled trial.' *Child Abuse & Neglect* *29*, 135–145.

Cohen, J. A., Mannarino, A. P., Berliner, L. and Deblinger, E. (2000) 'Trauma-focused cognitive behavioral therapy for children and adolescents: An empirical update.' *Journal of Interpersonal Violence* *15*(11), 1202–1223.

Cohen, J. A., Deblinger, E., Mannarino, A. P. and Steer, R. A. (2004) 'A multisite, randomized controlled trial for children with sexual abuse-related PTSD symptoms.' *Journal of the American Academy of Child & Adolescent Psychiatry* *43*(4), 393–402.

Cohen, J. A., Bukstein, O., Walter, H., Benson, R. S. *et al.* (2010) 'Practice parameter for the assessment and treatment of children and adolescent with posttraumatic stress disorder.' *Journal of the American Academy of Child & Adolescent Psychiatry* *49*(4), 414–430.

Cook, J. M., Schnurr, P. P. and Foa, E. B. (2004) 'Bridging the gap between posttraumatic stress disorder research and clinical practice: The example of exposure therapy.' *Psychotherapy: Theory, Research, Practice, Training* *41*(4), 374–387.

Copeland, W. E., Keeler, G., Angold, A. and Costello, E. J. (2007) 'Traumatic events and posttraumatic stress in childhood.' *Archives of General Psychiatry* *64*(5), 577–584.

De Arellano, M. A., Waldrop, A. E., Deblinger, E., Cohen, J. A., Danielson, C. K. and Mannarino, A. R. (2005) 'Community outreach program for child victims of traumatic events: A community-based project for underserved populations.' *Behavior Modification 29*(1), 130–155.

Deblinger, E., Steer, R. A. and Lippmann, J. (1999) 'Two-year follow-up study of cognitive behavioral therapy for sexually abused children suffering post-traumatic stress symptoms.' *Child Abuse & Neglect 23*(12), 1371–1378.

Deblinger, E., Mannarino, A. P., Cohen, J. A. and Steer, R. (2006a) 'A follow-up study of a multisite, randomized, controlled trial for children with sexual abuse-related PTSD symptoms.' *Journal of the American Academy of Child & Adolescent Psychiatry 45*(12), 1475–1484.

Deblinger, E., Mannarino, A. P., Cohen, J. A. and Steer, R. A. (2006b) 'A follow-up study of a multisite, randomized, controlled trial for children with sexual abuse-related PTSD symptoms.' *Journal of the American Academy of Child & Adolescent Psychiatry 45*(12), 1474–1484.

Deblinger, E., Mannarino, A. B., Cohen, J. A., Runyon, M. K. and Steer, R. (2011) 'Trauma-focused cognitive behavioral therapy for children: Impact of the trauma narrative and treatment length.' *Depression and Anxiety 0*, 1–9.

Deblinger, E., Mannarino, A. P., Cohen, J. A., Runyon, M. K. and Steer, R. A. (2011) 'Trauma-focused cognitive behavioral therapy for children: Impact of the trauma narrative and treatment length.' *Depression and Anxiety, 28*(1), 67–75.

DeVoe, E. R. (2009) 'Review of treating trauma and traumatic grief in children and adolescents.' *Child & Adolescent Social Work Journal 26*(3), 283–286.

Farmer, E. M. Z., Burns, B. J., Phillips, S. D., Angold, A. and Costello, E. J. (2003) 'Pathways into and through mental health services for children and adolescents.' *Psychiatric Services 54*(1), 60–66.

Finkelhor, D., Ormrod, R. K. and Turner, H. A. (2007) 'Re-victimization patterns in a national longitudinal sample of children and youth.' *Child Abuse & Neglect 31*(5), 479–502.

Foa, E. B. and Rothbaum, B. O. (1988) *Treating the Trauma of Rape: Cognitive-behavioral Therapy for PTSD.* New York, NY: Guilford Press.

Foa, E. B., Chrestman, K. R. and Gilboa-Schechtman, E. (2009) *Prolonged Exposure Therapy for Adolescents with PTSD: Emotional Processing of Traumatic Experiences: Therapist Guide.* Cambridge: Cambridge University Press.

Foa, E. B., Huppert, J. D. and Cahill, S. P. (2006) 'Emotional processing theory: An update.' In B. O. Rothbaum (ed.) *The Nature and Treatment of Pathological Anxiety* (pp.3–24). New York, NY: Guilford Press.

Folkman, S. and Moskowitz, J. T. (2004) 'Coping: Pitfalls and promise.' *Annual Review of Psychology 55*, 745–774.

Ford, J. D. (1978) 'Therapeutic relationship in behavior therapy: An empirical analysis.' *Journal of Consulting and Clinical Psychology 46*(6), 1302–1314.

Ford, J. D. and Cruz, M. (2006) *Trauma Affect Regulation: Guidelines for Education and Therapy; Adolescent/Pre-Adolescent Group Manual (TARGET-A).* Farmington, CT: University of Connecticut.

Garcia, J. A. and Weisz, J. R. (2002) 'When youth mental health care stops: Therapeutic relationship problems and other reasons for ending youth outpatient treatment.' *Journal of Consulting and Clinical Psychology 70*(2), 439–443.

Grasso, D. J., Joselow, B., Marquez, Y. and Webb, C. (2011) 'Trauma-focused cognitive behavioral therapy of a child with posttraumatic stress disorder.' *Psychotherapy 48*(2), 188–197.

Grasso, D. J., Cohen, L. H., Moser, J. S., Hajcak, G., Foa, E. B. and Simons, R. F. (2012) 'Seeing the silver lining: Potential benefits of trauma exposure in college students.' *Anxiety, Stress, and Coping 25*(2), 117–136..

Grasso, D., Greene, C. and Ford, J. D. (2013) 'Cumulative trauma in childhood.' In J. D. Ford and C. A. Courtois (eds) *Complex Trauma in Children.* New York, NY: Guilford Press.

Grasso, D. J., Webb, C., Cohen, A. and Berman, I. (2012) Building a Consumer Base for Trauma-Focused Cognitive Behavioral Therapy in a State System of Care. Administration and Policy in Mental Health. doi: 10.1007/s10488-012-0410-3

Greene, C., Grasso, D. and Ford, J. D. (in press) 'Emotion regulation in the wake of childhood complex trauma.' In J. C. Vogel and R. Pat-Horenczyk (eds) *Trauma and Resilience.* New York, NY: Routledge.

Harvey, S. T. and Taylor, J. E. (2010) 'A meta-analysis of the effects of psychotherapy with sexually abused children and adolescents.' *Clinical Psychology Review 30*(5), 517–535.

Henggeler, S. W. (1999) 'Multisystemic therapy: An overview of clinical procedures, outcomes, and policy implications.' *Child Psychology & Psychiatry Review 4*(1), 2–10.

Hobfoll, S. E. (1989) 'Conservation of resources: A new attempt at conceptualizing stress.' *American Psychologist 44*(3), 513–524.

Hobfoll, S. E. (2001) 'The influence of culture, community, and the nested-self in the stress process: Advancing Conservation of Resources theory.' *Applied Psychology: An International Review 50*(3), 337–370.

Imel, Z. E., Laska, K. M., Jakupcak, M. and Simpson, T. (2013) 'Meta-analysis of dropout in treatments for posttraumatic stress disorder.' *Journal of Consulting and Clinical Psychology 81*(3), 394–404.

Jaycox, L. H., Cohen, J. A., Mannarino, A. P., Walker, D. W. et al. (2010) 'Children's mental health care following Hurricane Katrina: a field trial of trauma-focused psychotherapies.' *Journal of Traumatic Stress 23*(2), 223–231.

Kazdin, A. E. and Kendall, P. C. (1998) 'Current progress and future plans for developing effective treatments: Comments and perspectives.' *Journal of Clinical Child Psychology. Special Issue: Empirically supported psychosocial interventions for children 27*(2), 217–226.

Kelley, M. L., Self-Brown, S., Le, B., Bosson, J. V., Hernandez, B. C. and Gordon, A. T. (2010) 'Predicting posttraumatic stress symptoms in children following Hurricane Katrina: A prospective analysis of the effect of parental distress and parenting practices.' *Journal of Traumatic Stress 23*(5), 582–590.

Lilienfeld, S. O. (2007) 'Psychological treatments that cause harm.' *Perspectives on Psychological Science 2*(1), 53–70.

Littleton, H., Horsley, S., John, S. and Nelson, D. V. (2007) 'Trauma coping strategies and psychological distress: A meta-analysis.' *Journal of Traumatic Stress 20*(6), 977–988.

Maiter, S., Palmer, S. and Manji, S. (2006) 'Strengthening social worker-client relationships in child protective services addressing power imbalances and "ruptured" relationships.' *Qualitative Social Work: Research and Practice 5*(2), 167–186.

Mannarino, A. P., Cohen, J. A., Deblinger, E., Runyon, M. K. and Steer, R. A. (2012) 'Trauma-focused cognitive-behavioral therapy for children: Sustained impact of treatment 6 and 12 months later.' *Child Maltreatment 17*(3), 231–241.

March, J. S., Amaya-Jackson, L., Murray, M. C. and Schulte, A. (1998) 'Cognitive-behavioral psychotherapy for children and adolescents with posttraumatic stress disorder after a single-incident stressor.' *Journal of the American Academy of Child & Adolescent Psychiatry 37*(6), 585–593.

McKay, M. M., Hibbert, R., Hoagwood, K., Rodriguez, J. et al. (2004) 'Integrating Evidence-Based Engagement Interventions Into "Real World" Child Mental Health Settings.' *Brief Treatment and Crisis Intervention Journal 4*(2), 177–186.

Morris, A., Gabert-Quillen, C. and Delahanty, D. (2012) 'The association between parent PTSD/depression symptoms and child PTSD symptoms: A meta-analysis.' *Journal of Pediatric Psychology 37*(10), 1076–1088.

Ozer, E. J., Best, S. R., Lipsey, T. L. and Weiss, D. S. (2008) 'Predictors of posttraumatic stress disorder and symptoms in adults: A meta-analysis.' *Psychological Trauma: Theory, Research, Practice, and Policy 1*, 3–36.

Resick, P. A. and Schnicke, M. K. (1992) 'Cognitive processing therapy for sexual assault victims.' *Journal of Consulting and Clinical Psychology 60*(5), 748.

Roberts, A. L., Galea, S., Austin, S. B., Cerda, M. *et al.* (2012) 'Posttraumatic stress disorder across two generations: Concordance and mechanisms in a population-based sample.' *Biological Psychiatry 72*(6), 505–511.

Rolfsnes, E. S. and Idsoe, T. (2011) 'School-based intervention programs for PTSD symptoms: A review and meta-analysis.' *Journal of Traumatic Stress 24*(2), 155–165.

Rosenberg, M., Schooler, C., Schoenbach, C. and Rosenberg, F. (1995) 'Global self-esteem and specific self-esteem: Different concepts, different outcomes.' *American Sociological Review 60*, 141–156.

Rutter, M. (2013) 'Annual research review: Resilience – clinical implications.' *Journal of Child Psychology and Psychiatry 54*(4), 474–487.

Schnider, K. R., Elhai, J. D. and Gray, M. J. (2007) 'Coping style use predicts posttraumatic stress and complicated grief symptom severity among college students reporting a traumatic loss.' *Journal of Counseling Psychology. Special Issue: Racial and ethnic identity theory, measurement, and research in counseling psychology: Present status and future directions 54*(3), 344–350.

Snell-Johns, J., Mendez, J. L. and Smith, B. H. (2004) 'Evidence-based solutions for overcoming access barriers, decreasing attrition, and promoting change with underserved families.' *Journal of Family Psychology 18*(1), 19–35.

Stein, B. D., Jaycox, L. H., Kataoka, S. H., Wong, M. *et al.* (2003) 'A mental health intervention for schoolchildren exposed to violence.' *JAMA: the Journal of the American Medical Association 290*(5), 603–611.

Taylor, S. E. and Stanton, A. L. (2007) 'Coping resources, coping processes, and mental health.' *Annual Review of Clinical Psychology 3*, 377–401.

Vervliet, B., Craske, M. G. and Hermans, D. (2013) 'Fear extinction and relapse: State of the art.' *Annual Review of Clinical Psychology 9*(1), 215–248.

Vogt, D. S., Rizvi, S. L., Shipherd, J. C. and Resick, P. A. (2008) 'Longitudinal investigation of reciprocal relationship between stress reactions and hardiness.' *Personality and Social Psychology Bulletin 34*(1), 61–73.

Watt, B. D. and Dadds, M. R. (2007) 'Facilitating treatment attendance in child and adolescent mental health services: A community study.' *Clinical Child Psychology and Psychiatry 12*(1), 105–116.

Woody, S. R., Detweiler-Bedell, J., Teachman, B. A. and O'Hearn, T. (2003) *Treatment Planning in Psychotherapy: Taking the Guesswork Out of Clinical Care.* New York, NY: Guilford Press.

Yeung, N., Holroyd, C. B. and Cohen, J. D. (2005) 'ERP correlates of feedback and reward processing in the presence and absence of response choice.' *Cerebral Cortex 15*(5), 535–544.